The Road to Rock

W. T. Schmidt

Table of Contents

Foreword

This book is about a fictitious rock-performing character named Wailing Wager. The book is based on this author's personal experience in Hollywood as a "sideman" for various singers and groups over the years. I would play on the side of the stage while the STAR would be the "frontman" performing on the front of the stage.

In talking with various successful rock artists over the years, I have obtained some very interesting stories. This includes how they were raised as a child, their unique introductions to music, developing their personal music skills, and finally, becoming a rock star. It was a long "ROAD" for most of them, hence the title of this book.

The main book character in this book is John "Wailing" Wagner. He is based on these multiple existing artists and their personal stories. I always found such stories fascinating on how they shaped the artist's performing skills of rock and roll. Their personal experiences are included in the book.

Chapter 1 – The Beginning

The term "small-town boy" has been utilized by authors for many years and applies to this book's main character, John Wagner. He was raised on an island in Puget Sound, Washington and schooled on the mainland in the city of Marion. John was certainly uneducated regarding the outside world, but he was musical. He played in the school band, sang in church choirs for years, and performed in school musicals. John could read sheet music and perform without practicing. As the saying goes among musicians, he could read "flypaper" with no mistakes. It was an easy "A" in the school band and choir. He even got to sing solos when performing at church at Christmas. He was enamored with recording artists and loved to sing along with them on the car radio or the family record player.

In the early winter of 1960, John got suckered into the Columbia Record Club even though he couldn't afford it with his small weekly $1.50 allowance. The Club's advertising said if he joined, he could get five "free" vinyl records. He chose records by Jimmie Rodgers, the Kingston Trio, and the Chad Mitchell Trio with some member named John Denver. He would listen and learn the lyrics while singing along with the records.

When it became close to Christmas, John's dad, Noel, asked what John wanted for Christmas, and John said a guitar. He wanted to play guitar and sing with the records he wasn't paying for. The music sounded like so much fun. Songs like "3 Jolly Coachmen", "MTA", "Honeycomb", and so on. Naturally, the records eventually stopped coming for lack of payment, but John would pay "something" with each monthly bill that he received.

By the time Christmas rolled around, John had forgotten about his guitar request. On Christmas morning, there was this long, narrow suitcase under the tree, and it had John's name on it. When it was John's turn to open it, his dad and mom looked at each other with a big grin; excited for John's reaction. He opened it, and inside was this beautiful yellow-looking thing with a guitar neck on it. John was confused and had to ask, "What is this?"

Noel was very surprised and said, "It's a guitar."

A guitar? John thought. It didn't look like a guitar. He strummed the strings, and there was hardly a sound. It didn't even have a hole in it. It said Fender Telecaster.

"Well … what do you think?" asked his dad.

"It doesn't have a hole in it. Guitars have a hole in the middle so that there is an echo sound from the strings."

"A hole?"

"Yeah, a hole right about here in the middle."

John's dad was mad! "Well, the music salesman said that this is a guitar that all the young people wanted. So, I bought it. Well … damn … we will go back to the store and see what's going on."

The next Monday, John and his dad drove the 50 miles to the music store in Lynnwood, Washington. When they walked in, the store had a bunch of guitars with "holes" in them hanging on the wall. So, John knew he was right. His dad walked up to the owner, Mac, who sold him the yellow guitar and said, "You sold me the WRONG GUITAR. This one doesn't make a sound." Mac smiled and said that the guitar was an electric guitar.

John thought that was wrong too, because it didn't have an electric cord coming out of it. John showed the salesman that there was no electric cord. Mac smiled again. "You need an amplifier. Let me show you". He took John's guitar, put a wire in it, and then plugged the wire into an amplifier box. He turned the box on, and the guitar (then) made a sound out of the box. Then, Mac played a simple tune on it to show how it worked.

He continued, "I told you that you would need an amplifier and a guitar cord, but you said you would get that later. I am sorry about the mix-up, but this is what you have". Noel said he wanted his money back, but the Mac pointed to the sign on the wall that said, "No Refunds". He could see John's dad was very mad. So, Mac started helping John with the concept of an electric guitar. "I'll tell you what. We will sell you a training "amp," and you can pay an extra $5 a month on your contract. I will also throw in some lessons with our guitar instructor for free when you are in the area."

So ... John was stuck with this "electric" guitar with no hole, and he had to pay for an amplifier. John asked Mac if the Kington Trio played an electric guitar, and he said, "No, but Chuck Berry and Buddy Holly do." Mac picked up the guitar, cranked up the volume on the amp, and wailed on a Chuck Berry lead guitar lick. WOW, that was exciting, thought John! All of a sudden, the Kington Trio wasn't that cool.

When John and his dad got home, John hooked up the guitar to the amplifier box like Mac showed him. He started picking on the strings with a "guitar pick." His dad was still pretty mad at the situation, and Noel told John never to play the guitar with the amplifier "turned on" when he was home. When he was home, John could still hear the strings a little bit without the amplifier, but when his dad was off working somewhere, he would crank up the amplifier with its three-inch speaker. Since there was nothing to do all winter except look at the rain, John would sit down at the radio and then try to play the guitar parts that he heard. When Noel went through Lynnwood, he would drop John off at the music store, and he would take a free lesson from the store instructor, Jerry Simon. The instructor taught John how to read guitar notes off of sheet music and music charts. Plus, he gave him some of his well-worn "Beginner's Guitar" books on how to read sheet music. John's background with sheet music in the school band and choir gave him the knowledge to read guitar music as well. Little did John know that when he got to Hollywood, the music industry had only a handful of guitar players who could "read" sheet music.

John kept practicing guitar while listening to the radio for months, and Jerry, his instructor, said John was getting "pretty proficient" at reading music. Luckily, Jerry kind of took John "under his wing" and continued to give him free lessons every once in a while when John could get to Lynnwood with his dad. Playing guitar was easy, with the strings tuned to play harmonies with just a strum. John could place his fingers on the guitar neck, as shown in the book and play all sorts of chords, whether it was E, F, G, etc. chords.

Chapter 2 – The Super 8

When John played the last football game of the season for his small high school, he had been elected captain. They had a good year. When the game was over, and the high school had won the league championship. John started running off the football field and looking for his mom and dad. John saw Noel walking onto the field, but not with Mom … it was Uncle Lloyd. His mom, Cora, had stayed home with John's younger brother and let Noel and his brother Lloyd come to the game. WOW … Uncle Lloyd had driven 60 miles from Seattle to see the game with John's dad. John was so surprised and so honored. Noel and Lloyd both congratulated John on the championship and told him they had a surprise once he got dressed. "A surprise," John thought. He knew that Uncle Lloyd had to leave to get home, so John showered and got dressed right away. He didn't celebrate in the locker room with all the players. John walked outside, where Noel and Lloyd were waiting, with smiles on their faces.

"We want to show you something."

The three of them walked out to the school parking lot, and there was Uncle Lloyd's old car; a 1941 Buick Super 8 coupe with its straight engine design.

"I want you to have this, John," said Uncle Lloyd. "I bought a new car and don't need this old one anymore. It runs okay. It can get you back and forth from school and home." John was blown away by this generosity.

John's dad continued, "You are insured to drive this car; everything is all taken care of. I have to drive Lloyd home and, so you can drive yourself home. It is a stick shift, but you know how to drive it. Just be careful of the clutch because it is 20 years old."

When Uncle Lloyd gave John the key, he shook Lloyd's hand with strong appreciation and said, "Thank you!" In those days, males did not hug each other, just a handshake.

As Noel and Lloyd walked away to Noel's car, John got inside the Super 8 and looked around. This car was kind of a legend in the Wagner family. Uncle Lloyd drove it all around the University of Washington campus as a young Dean. One day, he was driving up the "Ave" in the University District, and the Super 8 died. Some guy behind him started honking his horn. So, Uncle Lloyd got out and lifted up the hood. University Deans don't take auto-mechanical training, so he didn't know what to look for. In the meantime, the guy in the back kept honking his horn. Uncle Lloyd checked the spark plug wires and it didn't seem to help. The horn honker kept honking and so Lloyd went back to him and said, "I tell you what. You try and fix my car and I'll sit back here and honk the horn!"

The Super 8 had an ugly brown interior with a green dashboard, but it was now John's Car. Wow! After a couple of minutes, John got out, locked the car, and headed to the dance in the school cafeteria and… the school celebration. As usual, when he walked in the door, the girls ignored him. John always felt like a freak with his football dentures, his dad's home haircut, and acne. But … John did notice a couple of things that were a little different because of the championship. One or two girls actually looked at him.

John liked to dance to the rhythm of the music, but not many girls could move that well around the dance floor. It seemed they only wanted to "slow dance" with John. He asked a girl to dance, and while dancing slowly, she came in close to him, real close. Then she started stroking his hair and steering him over to where most of the girls sat. As they danced, John started to get… ah… excited, responding to her close body. When the music stopped, she suddenly pulled away from him in front of the girls, with all of them looking at his "belt buckle area". *Wow*, thought John, *what was all that about?*

As the girls started whispering among each other, one of them, Betty Jenson, got up and walked over to John and said, "Hello, captain."

"Captain?" He was caught off guard.

"Yes, captain. You are the captain of the football team. Right?"

"Oh… yeah… do you want to dance?"

"No… I have other ideas… do you have a car, John?"

"Yeah, I just got it tonight as a gift."

"Well… I have a gift for you. Let's go look… at your car… right now."

As they walked out the door to the parking lot, Betty grabbed John's hand, and he led her to the Super 8. John was going to show her the car, but she had other ideas.

"Let's get in the back seat… Captain."

The 20-year-old Super 8 had 20-year-old non-functioning shock absorbers, which caused the car to gently go up and down as they got to know each other in the backseat. John had to admit Betty knew her stuff, and she taught him a few things that night… that seemed to go on for an hour. When people started coming out of the dance, they stopped their fun and John took her home. He tried to kiss her goodnight at the door, but she pulled away with a big smile on her face.

"See you around… Captain"

When John went to school on Monday, all the guys started slapping him on the back with big grins, and most of the girls looked at him with "disdain". John wondered what that was all about. Unknown to him, Betty had started a phone campaign over the weekend, telling everyone about John's "Super 8" … and the backseat. That's when he learned that "people like to talk". So, from then on… John decided at a relatively young age to keep "his" mouth shut. He would never join in and participate in such gossip "with the guys". By Wednesday, the attitude of the school was back to normal, and John could breathe a little easier. That night, the crank phone rang in the drafty old log house … two long rings and three short ones. That was the family's ring. John's mom answered the phone and said, "It's for you, John". He picked up the earpiece and spoke into the collector.

"Hello." There was a long pause, but John could hear someone breathing over the line hum. He continued, "Who is this?"

Still a pause, and then she spoke, "This is Barbara Benson… John."

Oh My Gosh, thought John. Barbara was one of the most beautiful girls in the school. He was a little dumbfounded but was able to respond.

Oh… hello… what can I do for you… Barbara?"

"Why Betty… and not me?"

Oh, my goodness. John was caught flat-footed. *Think, John. Think, John.* "Well… you are going steady, right?"

"Why not me, John?"

He had to think fast. "I have always been interested in you. You know that. How many times have you caught me staring at you? Are you interested in getting together?"

"… maybe."

"Well… no one has to know unless you want someone to know. I keep my mouth shut… it would be just between you and me… what do you think?"

A long pause, and then, "Okay… but… where would we meet?"

"Anywhere you would feel safe… I don't care where. I would be looking at you … only."

"Okay… how about the cemetery?"

"The cemetery? Now, that would be a really romantic place".

Barbara started to laugh. John finally broke the log jam, and words started to flow between them. Barbara finally said, "Let's get together on Tuesday when the sun goes down. Say around 7?"

"I will meet you on the west side of the cemetery, away from the main road… this will be just between you and me, Barbara. Right?"

As John hung up the phone, his thoughts were going a mile a minute. Barbara had black hair and beautiful blue eyes that he just loved. This was going to be tricky. She was going steady with one of the richest guys at the school, and John had NOTHING but a 41 Buick. Still… both had exchanged glances at school all the time, but no staring. You never wanted your fellow students to catch on that you liked someone.

On Tuesday, when the sun went down, and it was close to seven o'clock, John pulled into the cemetery and went to the backside. There was Barbara's family car. As John got out of the Super 8, she opened her door and just sat there on the edge of the seat. Her interior light came on, and John could see her beauty.

"I think you should get out of your car and shut the door so the light will go off."

"Oh… yeah".

As she shut the car door, an auto started driving by on the main road and didn't stop. So far, so good. Any hint of this meeting would be all over the school if anyone found out. John didn't want to disrupt her life and… her steady boyfriend arrangement. At least not for now. He told her again that he would keep "my mouth shut," and she didn't have to worry about school gossip. John also explained his family's 15-party phone line and that if she called on that phone, she should use the name "Helen".

John could tell she was starting to get nervous and hesitant, so he began to press the situation.

"So … here we are … what do you have in mind?"

She stood there for a while and started to head for her car. "I have to go."

"What?!"

John had to think fast, and he gently grabbed her right wrist to stop her. He pointed to a headstone next to them.

"Look … there is Helga Olson … what would Helga think if you left?"

Barbara chuckled and stopped. John gently grabbed her other wrist and pulled her toward him, pressing her hard against his body, and she responded. She started kissing John uncontrollably all over his face and neck. John got excited and gently picked her up and carried her over to the Super 8.

At school the next day, John started looking for Barbara. He knew where her locker was and walked by a few times, but … no Barbara. Finally, after lunch, he caught sight of her with a few other girls at her locker. John casually walked by without looking at her and started muttering, "Helga, Helga." Barbara did a silly little laugh and kept talking to her girlfriends. John got the message, and he didn't try to talk to her. Her boyfriend was rich and had a new car. But … from time to time, John's family phone would ring, two long, three short, and his mom would say, "John, it's Helen."

Winter during John's senior year of high school was becoming boring with all the rain and fog and living in a "one-horse town" with nothing to do. John always had his guitar, but his dad wouldn't let him use the amp with its three-inch speaker. John had already read the music and learned just about all the tunes from the music books that Mac at the music store had given him. The books had songs such as "The Big Rock Candy Mountain", "You Are My Sunshine", "Tea For Two", etc. John decided to take some action and get out of this rut.

"Dad … when is the next time you are going to go through Lynnwood? I would like to go to that music store."

He answered, "Next Thursday."

When John's dad did go to Seattle, he had to drive right by the store. It was on Highway 99, the main road to Seattle from the north. There were no interstate highways in 1960, just roads that forced drivers to go through every little town like Lynnwood before getting to Seattle. So, on Thursday, John went with his dad. Noel dropped him off at the store. John would hang out at the store, and then his dad would pick him up on the way home.

When John walked into the store, Mac spotted him and said, "Hi, John. Are you here for another 'free lesson'?" as he laughed.

John said, "No, I just want to hang out and look around at your equipment and sheet music."

"Hey, you are really getting good at reading sheet music and one of Jerry's best students. You must practice quite a bit. Keep that up, and you will be working and getting paid."

John thought, *Getting paid for reading music? Huh?"* Just then, the door entrance "bonger" went off, and Mac went out front to see who was walking in the door.

It was a young guy in his 20s, and he seemed to know Mac. "Hi, Mac, how are you doing?"

"Well, Paul, good to see you. What brings you to my establishment? Did you break some more guitar strings?"

"Yeah, that's what I am here for."

Mac went behind the counter and pulled out a couple of packs of "flat wound" guitar strings.

"You break more guitar strings than any guitar player I know."

"Yeah, I break a lot. Are you going to start giving a quantity discount?"

Mac laughed and pulled out these "flat wound" strings that didn't make a sound when the player moved up and down the neck. They were almost double the normal cost of regular strings: $3.33.

John decided to walk up to where they were and take a look at a professional guitar player. He had a crew cut and wore jeans with a colorful red shirt. There was no appearance that would tell you he was a musician. Mac spotted John and introduced him to Paul.

"John, this is Paul Goddard, and he plays guitar for the group called the Tempos. Paul, this is John Wagner. John is one of my best sheet music readers of all Jerry's students." John shook Paul's hand, and Paul looked at John with curiosity. Paul made John feel like that was something odd, reading music.

"You can read sheet music?"

"Well, sort of …"

Mac started talking again, "So Paul, where are you playing lately?"

"I think we are playing the Beacon Ball Room on Friday and at Silvana on Saturday."

Mac was curious, "How much do you make when playing the off-road hall in Silvana?"

"I think we make about $25 a piece … something like that."

$25? John thought. *For one night's work? My gosh, they must play for a lot of hours to make that much money.*

Silvana was only about six miles from John's town and in the middle of nowhere. Maybe three businesses and the Viking Hall for area meetings and dancing. The dances at the Viking Hall funded the hall maintenance and the Viking Club expenses.

The hall offered live music and dancing every Saturday night for a one-dollar entrance fee. Paul continued to talk to Mac, "Do you have that new Fender guitar in yet?"

"Yeah, it's up there on the wall. Do you want to try it?"

Paul went over and picked it off the wall. He didn't say anything. He plugged it into an amplifier and started playing just like the records John had heard. He played differently than John. He moved up and down the neck with ease and hit every note correctly. "How much is this beauty, Mac?"

"$425."

"Whew … that's a few gigs, huh?"

John asked Paul how often he played at Silvana, and Paul said, "We play there about once a month. If you are ever at Silvana, look me up."

When Paul left, John went up to Mac and asked if he could show him how Paul was able to play up and down the guitar neck. Mac explained that Paul was using the rock and roll "bar chord" method. He asked John to play an E chord, and he complied. Mac began to explain this method.

"Now, take your left finger and cross over the whole neck and form an E chord above it. Good. That is now an F chord."

He showed how the bar chord being placed on the neck would form every chord that John already knew.

"The key is how you place the left-hand fingers on the low E string. It becomes the basis for all the chords on the neck. This is F, then G, A, B flat, B, C, D, and then the octave E chord here." Mac could see that John understood the concept. "Or … you can simply cover all the strings on the neck with your left-hand fingers and move up the neck for all the chords as well."

John suddenly realized that when he played a Pop Song in E, he could move up the neck to play the A chord and the B chord. AND … it sounded like the records on the radio.

Mac continued, "What Jerry has been teaching you up until now are big band and folk music chords that you originally wanted to know. If you want to learn the rock and roll chords, it will only take about an hour. Do you have the time?"

Since John's dad hadn't arrived back, John sat down with Mac, and he showed John how the rock and roll chords worked. It seemed too easy to be true.

"Now ... don't get caught up on these easy chords. You have developed the skill of playing notes and chords from sheet music. You can get a lot of work if you continue to develop that skill and not just learn the simple rock and roll chords. If you want to learn more rock and roll, come in a couple of times, and Jerry will have you up to par in no time."

When John's dad showed up, and they started for home, John began to daydream, wondering what it would be like to play rock and roll in a group and ... get paid $25 for a dance. John had to find out what this was "all about".

"Dad, is it okay if I go to Silvana Saturday night?"

"SILVANA? What would you want to do in Silvana?"

John was relieved. His dad hadn't heard about the Silvana dance hall with its bad reputation.

"Well, it's a place where I can go and dance and meet girls."

"Oh, sort of like your high school dances?"

John breathed a sigh of relief, "Yeah, I guess you could say that."

"Sure, if you want to go off to Silvana, it would be okay, but make sure you get home early so your mom won't worry."

John had heard a lot of stories about Silvana with drunken brawls in the parking lot, people coming up from Seattle and pulling knives on the locals. But, still, he wanted to see what it was like and hear Paul's group, the Tempos.

When they got home, John grabbed his guitar and practiced the bar chord with the movement up and down on the neck. Then John turned on a rock and roll radio station: KJR.

"Alright, you dudes and chickees. It's time to rock and roll."

On came a familiar tune, "Sea Cruise". John quickly grabbed his guitar and groped around with bar chords and discovered it started with an F chord. When the song changed chords, he groped around again and found that the second chord was a C. Then it went back to F. With the third change, it went to a D and then back to F. As the song continued, John could see a pattern of just three chords in this rock and roll tune. He was amazed at how easy it was to play by moving these bar chords up and down the neck.

When a guitar player hits that moment of understanding the rock and roll chords, it opens the door to a huge inventory of tunes. This would include tunes from Buddy Holly to Elvis, from little-known groups to hugely successful rock singers and bands. This included the local acts in the Seattle area, such as the Wailers, Frantics, Statics, Little Bill and the Blue Notes. John hit that moment flying and began practicing day and night and singing the tunes that he already knew from the radio. This included the first tune, Sea Cruise. John would start singing a tune and then figure out what the beginning chord was. From there, he could hear the three chord changes and move through each song with relative ease. *WOW*. John had to get to Silvana and hear the Tempos live.

Chapter 3 – The Silvana Dance Hall

John was nervous as he drove along the winding country road to Silvana. All the stories about the rough and tumble nature of the dance hall were in the back of his mind. Still, John had never heard of a live band, and he had to go there to see Paul and his band, the Tempos. John was anxious to hear what an electric guitar would sound like with a band. Was it as good as a song on the radio? Was it louder? What could he expect?

"Silvana—two miles," said the road sign. Nerves started really setting in, and John's stomach turned into knots with uncertainty and excitement. He was probably going to be the youngest person there at 17. Was someone going to pick a fight? Was a person from Seattle going to pull a knife on him? Half of him was ready to turn around and go home to the safety of watching television. Then, after what seemed like an eternity, John pulled into the Silvana city limits.

The town was a little bigger than he had remembered. It was at least two blocks of farm buildings and a couple of retail stores. John slowly drove through the town to see if anyone was on the two corners with knives. He was relieved to see no one on the street. Everyone was inside the dance hall. John turned around and drove through the town an additional time to confirm the situation and then parked the Super 8. As he walked up to the door of the hall, John could hear the band wailing away inside.

When he opened the door, a huge man stood before him.

"It's $1.50 tonight, kid."

A $1.50 John thought. The school dances were 25 cents. Luckily, he had a couple of dollars and handed them to this big guy. He looked at John with curiosity. "Your new here, right?"

"Yeah."

"Now, here are the rules, kid—no booze, no fighting, no weapons inside. You can only smoke in the break area and don't put them out on the floor. Use the ashtrays. So … take at easy and have a good time."

As John walked in, the pulsating beat of the band immediately drove into his very being. It was like the music was being absorbed by his entire body. John's sensors were all on heightened alert. His thought pattern was going all across the board. He could feel the drums banging against his chest. The bass guitar penetrating his bones, the saxophone screaming in his ears. John could hear the piano a little bit and Paul playing the rhythm on his guitar.

When John entered the dance area, he could see about 300 people crammed into the hall that was actually meant for 100. They were all dancing away and didn't notice John as he inched up toward the front of the stage. The band was stepping back and forth to the rhythm of the music as they played, and it looked "cool." John started watching Paul on guitar as he moved his hands effortlessly up and down the neck of his guitar. When he played a featured guitar "lead", it sounded just like the song's record. John thought he had to be one of the best guitar players in the country. He wondered why Paul was playing Silvana and not New York or Hollywood.

All of a sudden, a fight broke out in the back of the dance hall. John couldn't see who it was with all the people dancing in front of the fighters. The huge bouncer came onto the dance floor and picked up the two under each arm, carrying both outside with them, still trying to wail away at each other and the bouncer. The crowd didn't even stop dancing. The band didn't even stop playing. Hardly anyone looked at the fight. This, of course, got John nervous again and so he went over to the corner below the stage. John stood on the stage steps to see where the sheriff's deputies and the bouncer were. The deputies were in each back corner with the bouncer at the front door. John felt a little more at ease when the lights came on, and the Tempos started playing Louie-Louie. Paul walked up to the microphone to speak.

"All you dudes and chickees, it is time for a break. We are the Tempos from Everett. We are going to take a 15-minute break, so take care of yourselves. We want our clientele back here on the dance floor in … 15 MINUTES.”

Paul then stepped back from the microphone a little and started singing, “Louie-Louie, oh oh oh, ME GOT GO,” and the band stopped playing. John laughed as the crowd filed out of the hall and into the drizzling rain in the parking lot to cool off. John wanted to talk to Paul and waited for him to come off the stage. All the players came down, but Paul went into a side room off the stage. John wondered if he should go back and find Paul. John finally built up enough nerve and entered the room.

“Hey, no one is allowed back here—just the band”, said Paul.

John gulped and said, “But Paul, my name is John Wagner, and I was at Mac’s when you came in to get some strings. You invited me to come and hear you play sometime.”

I did—oh, oh, yeah, you were the kid that can read music, right?”

“Yeah, that’s right.”

“So, you made it up here from Seattle?”

“No, I live locally and thought I’d stop by and hear you play.”

"You live here and go clear to Lynnwood for lessons? Well … you are to be commended for driving all that way to learn how to read music. How are you coming?"

"Okay, I guess. I know a lot of chords lower on the neck."

Paul smiled and looked at John. Paul could tell he saw a lot of himself in John when he first started playing guitar. "Do you want to sit in, sit in and play with the band?"

"Oh … I don't know … I have never played with a band before, and I don't have my guitar with me."

"You can use mine if you want."

"I only know about three songs."

"Which one do you want to play?"

John couldn't believe it! The nerves hit his stomach again. "About the only tune I know is Sea … Cruise …"

"Can you sing it too?" asked Paul."

"I don't know … Paul …"

Paul could see John's scared face, and he let John off the hook. "I tell you what. Why don't you have Mac teach you Louie-Louie and come back with YOUR guitar next time? We will be back here in 4 weeks. I really don't think you're ready to play with a band tonight, right?"

"Ah … no".

Paul smiled and could tell John was much relieved.

John felt more relaxed and sat down across from Paul as he cleaned up his guitar and wiped the sweat off of it. Then John heard a soft, feminine voice.

"Are you there, Paul?"

"Yeah, come on in."

John was still looking at Paul and his guitar when the girl walked in. "Captain … what are you doing here?"

John turned to see Betty standing in front of him. Paul was curious about Betty's comment. "Captain? What's this captain bit?"

"Well, honey, John's the captain of our football team."

"No kidding. A guitar-playing football captain … that's something else," Paul said with a smile.

John was not comfortable, but Betty was calm, cool, and collected. She smiled and said, "Would you excuse us, John, for a little bit?"

"Oh … sure … yes," and John walked out of the stage break room. He wasn't used to that. He was usually the first priority with Betty. But … John could understand Paul being in the band. He wasn't jealous or upset, just a little surprised with it all.

As John walked across the dance floor, he was amazed at how empty the hall looked, with only about 20 or so people still remaining inside. He continued walking into the break area and looking to buy a Coke or a Pepsi. Even the break area looked empty compared to the hall just a couple of minutes prior. John walked up to this older woman who looked about 23 and was running the concession area.

She looked at John and said, "What do you want?"

"I'll have a Pepsi or a Coke."

"That's 35 cents."

"WHAT? 35 cents?!" John said.

"Yeah, 35 cents. Do you have it or not?!"

"Well … yeah, I have it, but isn't that a little steep?

"Look it. We have overhead to run this place. Just give me the 35 cents!"

John thought this had to be the most expensive Pepsi that he had ever drunk in his life. John walked to a table and sat down. Then, a guy a couple of tables over began to talk.

"You're John Wagner, right?"

"Yeah, that's right." John looked him over and had no idea who he was.

"You played football for Marian High, right?"

"Yeah, that's right."

"I knew it … I played against you with Arlington."

"Oh… yeah … Arlington has always had a good football team."

"But … you beat us finally. So … are you going to stay here very long?"

"I don't know … I came to listen to the band."

The guy got up and walked over to the 10-cent pay phone on the wall to call someone.

John drank his Pepsi and decided to go outside to see what was going on. As he walked to the door, it opened, and a flood of people began coming back inside. John figured the break was about over and went back to the edge of the stage. As he walked by the stage break room, he could faintly hear familiar sounds being uttered by Betty inside.

Oh, brother, he thought. *Betty does get around.* He held no animosity towards her in any way, shape, or form. Simply amazed at her uniqueness compared to other girls. When Betty came out of the stage room, her hair was all messed up, and her dress wrinkled. She calmly walked up to John as if nothing had happened and said, "Well, Captain, who is your date tonight?"

John smiled and shook his head. "I'm going stag tonight, Betty. I basically came here to listen to Paul's guitar playing."

Betty smiled. "Well, what do you think? Are you going to get into music?"

"I don't know Betty, but I hope so. Paul has invited me to play with his group in four weeks when their back here, and I am anxious to give it a try."

"Boy, that would be great," said Betty. "Someone from Marian being in a rock and roll band."

Just then, the Tempos blasted into their first song after the break. Betty immediately turned around and began staring up at Paul as if John didn't exist. Again, the music pulsated through John's body. He fell back into a concentrated fog bank to where nothing existed around him except the music and Paul's playing. After what he thought was about half an hour, he looked at his watch, and it said 11 PM.

Oh no, John thought, *I have to head for home.*

He asked Betty if she needed a ride home, and she shook her head "No" and again started staring up at Paul. So, John started squeezing through the crowd to the front door. Suddenly, all the lights in the hall came on. One of the deputies pushed through the crowd to the switches and turned most of them off again. John thought, "What was all that about?"

He finally got to the door and stepped outside. There was the usual slight drizzle of rain that would cool off the crowd when they went outside on break. The fresh blast of outside air compared to the hall's cigarette smoke woke John up. As he started walking to the Super 8, he understood why so many people would come to Silvana and get away for three or four hours and forget their problems.

"Hey, Wagner," a voice shouted. "Come over here for a second. I want to talk to you."

"No, I have to get going and head for home." John noticed it was the guy from Arlington that he talked to briefly on break. "Ah, come on over for a couple of minutes and talk about the football game a little."

So … John decided to amble over to him in the parking lot where he was standing.

"There is someone I want to introduce to you."

Just then, Shurman, who John hurt in football, and two of his buddies stepped out from behind the parked cars. John's immediate response was to run, but two more guys were blocking his way.

"You really leveled me, Wagner, on that kickoff." John said nothing. "In fact, you gave me a concussion."

John said nothing but gave a little Steve McQueen smile … just a little.

"Do you realize how much pain you put me through in a 24-hour period?"

Again, John said nothing and pulled his dentures out of his mouth and showed what Shurman had done to him the year prior.

Shurman laughed and said, "Well, that's the spoils of football."

John finally started to speak, "Well, your concussion was spoils, too, Surhman."

Surhman looked mad, "I thought we would just show you what a concussion was like if you don't mind. We thought we would stomp your head and maybe break your nose … what do you think?"

John chose his words carefully. "So, that means all 5 of you having fun?"

Shurman smiled, "How about that? Wagner can count."

Then, a sixth person walked out from behind another car and walked inside the circle formed by the five guys around John. This new guy just stood next to John and spoke to the five. "You guys from Arlington aren't playing this too fair."

Shurman looked surprised. "Burns, this guy is from Marian … not Marysville.

Burns smiled and said, "Well, Marian is kind of close to Marysville, and five against one makes it even closer."

"We don't have any complaints with you. Why don't you leave this thing alone."

Burns made a glance at John and spoke in a soft voice. "I hope you're good because we are going to have a peck of fun in a couple of seconds." John just smiled at him. Burns continued in a low voice to John, "See the guy in the red shirt? He will try to kick you in the balls. The guy in green will try to slug you in the gut. I'll take Shurman and the other two."

Shurman was impatient. "Okay, Burns, you asked for it."

For a few seconds, which seemed like an eternity, it was a Mexican standoff. All of them just sized up each other, with Burns and John inside the circle of five guys. Burns and John stood in a back-to-back position facing out toward the circle of 5. Then Shurman yelled, "Get'em."

John quickly braced for the kick to his balls. When the guy tried to kick, John lifted his right foot and stomped on his shin, blocking the blow. The guy immediately went down in pain. The second guy came in for his punch to the gut, and John blocked it, grabbed his belt and picked him up off the ground. When John got him over his head, he threw the guy to the pavement on his back. He groaned and didn't move. When John turned around to help Burns, all he could see were three more bloody guys on the ground with Burns standing over them and yelling, "This is the most fun I have had in the past minute! You guys are real hard noise street fights, aren't you!"

The five of them just lay on the ground and said nothing. Burns continued, "Now I don't want to hear any more of this five-on-one crap. If you have a bone to pick with someone, you do it one-on-one. YOU GOT THAT?!"

Then Burns and John walked away. As they walked through the parking lot, John asked what his name was.

"Burns."

"No, what is your first name?"

"Ah … everyone just calls me Burns."

"Well, okay, thanks a lot … Burns."

"Think nothing of it. I guess you are pretty good at street fighting, too."

"Well … your tips about those two guys helped a lot."

"Yeah, some guys never learn anything new. Do you want a beer? I always have beer after work."

John had never had a beer before. He didn't want to seem ungracious, hence said, "Sure, why not."

"We'll go to my car," said Burns. "I hope you like Rainier."

John didn't want to let on that it would be his first beer and said, "It sounds great to me."

As they got into Burn's car, he handed John a sealed can of Rainier. "Get the church key out of the glove box."

"The church key?'

"You know … the can opener."

In those days a can of beer was sealed tight and had to be opened with a can opener that punched a hole in it, no pull tabs. John punctured his can and gave Burns … the church key. John decided to confess his status and said, "You know, this is my first street fight."

"Oh, my God, you're kidding."

"Nope … and … this is my first beer."

Burns put his beer on the dashboard and grabbed John's shoulder. "Son, you are really learning a lot tonight, huh? Have you ever been to Silvana before … well, let me guess, this the first time as well, right?"

"Yeah."

"Boy, you were really Christened tonight. If that was the first street fight you've been in, you are really going to develop those skills."

"Well … I am not really interested in fighting. I just got roped into it by Shurman."

"To tell you the truth, one, I get upset, and I kind of lose my head … you know what I mean?"

"I APPRECIAT THAT, Burns," and they both laughed hard.

Burns asked what John thought of his first beer. John didn't like it but said, "It's okay… I won't get drunk, will I?"

Burns smiled again, "ON ONE BEER? Boy, you are new at this. You know, it's time to make you into a man. Why don't you follow me in your car? We'll park somewhere and finish off this half-case before you go home?"

John smiled and said, "Okay."

Burns took them to some secluded spot; they drank beer and got to know each other. As the night progressed, the beer took its effect. A true bond started building between them, and developing a friendship that John had never experienced with anyone before. It became a friendship that still exists to this day. Finally, around two o'clock they finished the half case of beer.

"Well, Johns," said Burns, "It was niche meetin' ya. I'm gonna go. Look me up in da Marry'sville ponebook. I am the only Burns."

John looked at him with a smile and said, "I don feel sho good."

"Well … deres a busch over sthere. Can you smake itch out of my car and to dat busch?"

John opened the car door and ran to the bush and did his thing.

When John woke up in his bed the next morning, he wondered how he got home. His head was beating like the Tempos base drum. "This must be a hangover", he thought. Oh, John felt terrible.

John's Mom started yelling to him up in his sleeping loft, "John, are you up? You have to sing in church. What time did you get in, anyway?"

John stumbled out of bed and said, "I didn't look, Mom."

"Okay, did you have a good time?"

"Yeah, a very good time."

When John walked into the kitchen and his mom saw him, she was aghast. "John, you look horrible. Are you sick?"

"I don't know, mom. I have a headache, and my stomach is upset."

John's dad was sitting at the table and surveyed John carefully. "Honey, he probably has a slight bought of the flue. Right ... John?"

"Yeah, Dad, I think so."

"Cornelia, he will be fine in a matter of half a day or so. Is this the first time you've got this ... 24-hour flu, John?"

John figured Dad had figured. "Yeah, Dad, I think so."

"Well ... maybe we should talk about this when you come back from the church ... huh?"

John ate as much breakfast as he could. He wished his mom would stop banging the pots and pans around in the sink. When John got up to get dressed, his mom was concerned.

"John, you hardly touched your food. If you are sick, why don't you go back to bed."

"No, Mom, I have to sing a solo in church."

Chapter 4 – Getting Ready to Rock

Over the next three weeks, John started getting ready to play with the Tempos. He had Mac teach him Louie-Louie and a couple of other tunes, just in case. John practiced as much as he could, and when Dad was gone, he got out the guitar amplifier with its three-inch speaker and played through it. John wished he had a microphone so he could see what it was like singing through a mike. Finally, "The Night" came to play with the Tempos, and John headed to Silvana with his Fender Telecaster guitar. When John walked in, Paul greeted him with a smile.

"So … you want to be a rock and roll star tonight. Did you practice Louie-Louie like I told you? Are you going to sing it?"

"Mac showed me the chords … yeah, I think I'm ready to play and sing."

Paul faced the group. "Okay, guys. Let's do a little run-through with John before the crowd shows up. He has never sung with a group before. We will do it in the usual key of G. Is that right, John?"

"Yes, the key of G." I am sure Paul was a little apprehensive backing John up on his first try.

The piano started banging out the beginning chords, and then the drums and bass guitar came in with their usual force.

John could not believe the power that their playing instilled in him. His adrenalin was pumping beyond measure as he walked up to the mike to sing. When John began to sing, he sang it just like the record. All the practicing had paid off. As far as John was concerned, he was performing the record and really got into it.

John looked over at Paul; and his mouth was slightly open, and he had a puzzled look on his face. He kept staring at John like he was looking for a mistake or something. When they finished Louie-Louie, John looked over at Paul as if to say, "What do you think?"

Paul looked at him and said, "Well, it sounded pretty good, John. We'll give you a shot tonight with an audience. Are there any other songs you want to do tonight?"

"Yeah, Mac taught me Ginger Snap and Sea Cruise." Again, Paul was surprised because Ginger Snap was a lot more than just three chords.

"What are the keys for those two?"

"Key of G. Mac taught me everything in the key of G."

"Okay, guys, let's give John a shot at Ginger Snap. 1, 2, 3, 4 …"

When they started Ginger Snap, everything fell into place again. It was just like the record. The Tempos players were blasé, but John added something extra with his voice. The band just thought John was a friend of Paul's sitting in and not really a first-timer. When they finished Ginger Snap, John knew it was okay. He asked Paul if they could try Sea Cruise even though people were starting to file into the hall.

He said, "Oh, I guess so. Guys, just play a couple of verses."

They launched into Sea Cruise, and before the end of the 1ˢᵗ verse, the small group of people started dancing and looking at John's singing. John could tell Paul was surprised by his singing. All he was doing was just trying to sing like the record. That's all John had to go by. When they finished the practice, Paul called his guys over, away from John and talked to them quietly about John's playing and singing. All they did was nod their heads.

Later, during the dance when the second set began, after the break, Paul went up to the microphone and introduced John to the crowd. "We have a guest singer tonight—a good buddy of mine that I want you to know and hear. His name is John Wagner. Come on up, John."

When John came up on stage, the dancers simply milled around, hardly giving him a glance as if to say, "No big deal." John didn't say anything and nodded to the piano player to start playing Louie-Louie. As soon as the audience heard the beginning piano chords, they ran to get a partner to dance with.

When the band kicked in with the total sound, the whole place started jumping to this favorite dance tune.

Again, John didn't have anything to go by except the record. So, he just tried to sing like the singer on the record, Rock'n Robin Roberts. The crowd started looking up at him with curiosity. The power of playing and singing for a crowd was like a narcotic to John. He wanted more and more. John was in seventh heaven. By the time the band finished Ginger Snap and John started singing Sea Cruise, the crowd was going wild with yells, stomping, and extra dance movements. When Sea Cruise ended, they kept stomping their feet, wanting more. So … the Tempos played it a second time.

After the dance was over, Paul told John with a smile that he was surprised and a little jealous of the crowd's reaction. Paul said he saw the crowd fall for John after just three songs and started thinking of economics. Maybe utilizing John as a stand-up drawer for bigger dances in the future. John, of course, was shocked at that statement. However … Paul felt John couldn't use his actual name. He thought John should be given a stage name that would draw in people.

"Really?" John thought.

Paul stared off into space for a couple of minutes and said, "How about Wailing Wagner?"

John didn't know what to think and said, "Well … . okay. You know about crowds and what they like. I don't." John didn't think he was much of a "Wailing Wagner" at age 17, but if it would draw in people, he was willing to do anything to play and sing with Paul and the Tempos.

Chapter 5 – Wailing Wagner

When John went to school on Monday, he noticed that no one asked him about playing and singing at the Silvana dance hall. John figured no one was there. Silvana was not cool in high school. That was where the "misfits" went to drink and dance. That was okay. John didn't want to play with the Tempos to gain popularity. He just wanted to play and have fun.

Paul had given John a list of "suggested songs" for him to learn. They were composed of really wild songs by Chuck Berry, Freddie Cannon, Little Richard, and other similar wild music acts. John took the list to Mac at the music store, and he asked if Mac could get the sheet music with the cords and words. Mac laughed and said, "Sure, I can get it, but it will cost you close to $50".

John protested, "$50?! Why so much money?"

Mac laughed again and said that printed sheet music was not cheap. Everyone must make some money on each sale: the composer, the publisher, the wholesaler, and, of course, Mac's store. This was John's first introduction to the reality of the business side of music. Mac said he would order the sheet music, but some of it would have to come in from the East Coast, which would take over two weeks. Mac would need to send the order to each publisher or wholesaler by mail and the music would then be mailed through the post office back to the store. Mac said he would make all the orders, and John could pay for it when they came in. John said go ahead but wasn't quite sure how he was going to pay for it. John's Columbia Record Club experience was going to be utilized again.

Later, John called Paul and told him about his monetary plight. Paul laughed and said, "Just buy the record of each song and learn it off the record." Once John was off the phone with Paul, he called Mac at the music store and canceled his sheet music order. Mac was okay about it and said, "You probably talked to Paul, right?"

So, a couple of days later, John went to a record store in Seattle with his dad and discovered records of a single song where a dollar a piece. An album with 12 songs on it was $4. John couldn't afford many "singles," so he bought three "singles" (records/songs) with an advance on his allowance from his Dad. John could tell Dad was a little perturbed with his request for the $3 advance, but he did it for John. "Thanks, Dad."

The three songs were great dance songs. They were "Dear, Dad" by Chuck Berry, "My Wife Can't Cook" by Lonnie Russ, and a Freddie Cannon song about the South. All were what John called "rock'em sock'em" songs that dancers loved to dance too. The songs were really easy for him to learn, with just a few guitar chord changes. However, John also had to learn the "words" (lyrics) of each song. Learning and memorizing a song's lyrics was always time-consuming. The reason was that it was sometimes difficult to understand the singer's word pronunciations on the record. None of the musicians John played with over the years EVER appreciated his effort to learn, memorize, and sing the lyrics.

As John was learning these songs for the Silvana "gig," he got a call from Paul.

"Hi, John … say, I was wondering if you could go to a KJR Radio battle of the bands with me? It is this weekend, and I want you to hear the best groups in the State." A "battle of the bands" was when several groups played one after the other and battled for the attention of the dancers.

John was apprehensive, "I don't know if my car can make it to Seattle, but … I would love to go with you."

"Can you make it to Everett? If so, I will drive from there." John said he would try and drive slowly with his "struggling" Buick Super 8.

That night, John drove slowly to Everett, and he took off with Paul for Seattle on Highway 99 through Lynnwood. The battle of the bands was at a place called Parker's Ballroom, and kids were already lining up before they arrived there. This was a huge place that made Silvana look like a chicken coop. John wondered how many dancers the building could hold at one time. The performing groups were the best in the State of Washington. They were the Frantics, the Wailers, and the Dynamics.

When they got up to the ticket booth, the sign said $3.00! Ah, oh … all John had was $2.00, and he told Paul. Paul said he would pay the difference and take it out of John's pay in two weeks. John asked how much he was going to get paid for singing, and Paul said $10.00 to start. $10.00 was a lot better than nothing and so John accepted Paul's invitation.

When they got inside the ballroom, Paul walked over to the stage where one of the bands was setting up. When they both stopped in front of the stage, the guitar player looked up and smiled.

"Well, I'll be darned! Why, Paul, how are you doing?"

"Oh, as best that can be expected, Ron … Say, John, this is the guitar player for the Frantics, Ron Peterson."

As John shook Ron's hand, he knew that this guy was one of the most creative guitarists in the area. He had heard him play many guitar parts on the radio with several Billboard 100 tunes, such as Fog Cutter and Werewolf. Ron came up with guitar "licks" (guitar leads) that no one had thought of prior. This was especially true with his playing on Fog Cutter.

Ron looked at John and said, "Do you play guitar, John?"

"Well … a little bit … I'm just learning right now… how to play rock and roll."

"So, are you going to start using Paul's old trick … watching and stealing my licks," Ron said with a smile.

John looked over at Paul, and he began to laugh. "Yeah, I guess that is what we are here for. John has only been playing a short time but has great potential. That's why I brought him here to see you, Rich, and Larry."

Ron began to chuckle a little. "So, you want to be a guitar player, huh, John? It's a lot of fun if you like travel, not getting any sleep, low pay, and working with three other prima donnas."

Paul laughed and said, "Take it easy on him, Ron."

Ron smiled and continued to set up the rest of the band's equipment. John looked at the Frantic's band equipment, and it was staggering. Paul noticed John's interest and started explaining what all the stage equipment pieces were for. As Paul went through the list of equipment, John wondered how much all of it would cost and how he was going to pay for his equipment when only earning $10 a night with Paul.

When the Frantics began to play, they were fabulous. Every song they played sounded just like their record. John wondered what tours they went on to promote their records.

When they were done, another local group called the Wailers started setting up. John noticed that Paul "pulled back" from the stage and went into the background of the hall. Paul noticed the puzzled look on John's face, and he told him that the lead guitar player, Rich Dangle, didn't like to talk with other guitar players, especially when setting up equipment. When the Wailers started to play, they were LOUD and unique, and they played their own songs. The most famous song was Louie Louie, sung by their singer Rock'n Robin Roberts. A number of years later, a Portland group recorded the song in their garage. This was the Kingsmen group, and their version of Louie Louie went national across the United States.

The last group to set up at Parker's was the Dynamics. They had a larger than usual group of players, complete with a horn and sax. Paul immediately walked up to the edge of the stage. John followed him and wondered if they were going to talk to the lead guitar player, Larry Coryell. Larry was pretty busy, and Paul started talking to John.

"This guitar player is very talented. He can even play jazz. I have to really watch closely to get a grasp of the chords he is playing. He probably will be heading to New York in the near future and starting his own jazz act."

"Jazz?" John thought. He heard a jazz song called "Take Five", but he wasn't sure what a Jazz group would play or how you could make a living playing jazz; no dancing? When Larry Coryell came out on stage, he had a huge hollow "big box" guitar that was 50% larger than John's! When he started playing, John could see what Paul was talking about. The cords didn't sound the same. They weren't major or minor cords. WOW! John wondered if he had to learn these from Mac at the music store. John asked Paul, and he said, "No, the tempos just want to play top 40 tunes for dances. No jazz cords or licks."

When the Dynamics ended and the crowd started to leave, Paul had to struggle to get out of the Parker's Ballroom parking lot. Paul started talking about all the facets of the evening, which included music style, presentation, appearance, overall sound, etc. John felt he could understand most of what Paul was saying. Paul was a good teacher. He could present his opinions in "lay language" for a 17-year-old kid who didn't know much. This allowed John to pick up pivotal information about playing guitar with other musicians in the future.

"So … as you can see … we have a long way to go before we will be playing at Parker's. It is going to take a "boatload" of work, John. Do you want to do this as Wailing Wagner?"

John didn't know what to think. He just went along for the ride, "I guess so … what will I have to do?" he asked hesitantly.

"You're going to have to learn about 20 songs … You will need to learn to dance on stage while you are singing … You will have to buy some 'professional clothes' for performances on stage … AND … you will have to stay up later than 11 PM."

WOW! There certainly was a lot for John to think about as a greenhorn kid.

Chapter 6 – Getting It Together

Somehow, in some way, John was able to learn 20 "Rock'em Sock'em" songs to play and sing with the Tempos. They started using him about 50% of the time with their dances. John asked why they didn't use him all the time and Paul said that some dance halls weren't like Silvana. Those halls wanted more of a sophisticated sound instead of just rock and roll. John said he understood that. In actuality, the Tempos charged dance halls $25 extra dollars if Wailing Wagner was to perform, and these "sophisticated" halls wouldn't pay extra for John. John didn't know that. Though the Tempos only paid him $10 a night, the band did haul John around since the Super 8 wasn't dependable.

After about a year of singing and playing dances and graduating from high school in 1961, John wanted to move on. He told the Tempos he was heading to college and couldn't play with them anymore. John wanted to go to Bellingham, Washington, and attend Western Washington State College. Paul offered to give John a raise. Paul tempted John with $20 a night if he would continue! John said no. Paul was a little upset, but John gave Paul 30 days' notice.

When John first started attending Western, it was a true adjustment. He had never "lived on his own." John had a "stash" of money that he earned working at a frozen food factory during the summers starting at age 14. So, he was able to live in a dormitory on campus. When John arrived on campus, he was walking around and figuring out where everything was. All of a sudden, a guy came over and stopped Him.

"You're Wailing Wagner, Right?"

"Yeah"

"Are you still singing with the Tempos?"

"No … I moved up here to Bellingham, and I didn't like the 100-mile commute."

The guy didn't say anything … he just "looked John over," which seemed kind of weird. As John started to go, he grabbed John's arm. "Do you have a group up here, or are you going to start your own band?" That was a shock. John had no idea how "to start a band," and he said no.

The guy smiled and said, "I know someone you should meet. He is learning guitar and would be willing to start a band."

John was kind of dumbstruck, "I don't know how to do that. All I ever did was sing with the Tempos. I didn't handle the business side of things or tell the players what to do."

As John started to walk away again, the guy literally got in front of John and said, "How can I get in touch with you? Are you staying at the old or new dormitory?" John told him about the old dormitory and walked away. Wow, that was nuts!

The Western Washington College campus was beautiful. With all the rain, the grounds were very green and tall trees everywhere. John attended the school enrollment meeting the next day for freshmen and looked over the courses that he could take. In those days, there were no counselors to help students. John looked over a booklet that suggested courses for a "Pre-Major" if you didn't know what area you wanted to major in. One thing John had to take was "Bonehead" English due to his horrible score on the English section of the college entrance exam. John also chose a psychology course and a history course to start his college career. Not too impressive, but hopefully safe. In those days, if you "flunked out," you were drafted into the Army. The Vietnam War had already claimed the lives of three guys in his small hometown.

When John started "Bonehead" English, he discovered some amazing things. The word "are" is plural and the word "is" is singular; wow, amazing. He suddenly realized that his small-town high school education was going to be a handicap at Western; at least the first year. In history, he learned the world was not "flat" and that he had an "ego" in psychology. Boy ... John had to work to keep up and compete with other students. He went to the college bookstore, and they had some books that tutored him on the various scholastic "weaknesses" that he now knew he had to overcome. Luckily, hard work was never a problem with John, and he got caught up with everyone in a matter of three months. Unfortunately, half his fellow high school graduates who went off to college flunked out the first year!

After a couple of months at Western, John began to miss his Fender Telecaster and the three-inch speaker amp. His mom told him to come home for Thanksgiving. When John went back to school, he brought his guitar and amp. So, John started practicing again during the day when no one was in the dorm. He kept the volume down so as not to upset the dorm mom.

One day, there was a knock on the door, and this guy asked if John played guitar. He said, "Yes," and they both just stood there. At first, as John just stood in the doorway, the guy didn't say his name. John asked what he wanted, and the guy finally began to talk.

"I played a little guitar and was thinking of starting a group. A friend of mine said you played with a group down South, and … I was wondering if you would like to try forming a group?"

John was cautious, "I don't know how to form a group. I am interested in playing with a band because I need money to get through college."

He asked, "What kind of music John knew how to play?"

John said popular music off records and the radio. The guy suggested that maybe they should play together a little to see what it would be like. So, over the course of a couple of weekends, they discovered that they could play together and that … maybe they could put a group together. The guy knew a novice bass player in Ferndale, and John knew of a young snare drummer attending his old High School. Who knew if it would work? So, they all got together and started practicing with 32 miles of separation between each player. The 16-year-old snare drummer had great parents and allowed him to drive the distance for practices. The bass player and other guitar player drove together from Ferndale. John had the Super 8 that was starting to make "a lot of noise."

Over the course of a couple of months, they were able to practice at a meeting hall that was a converted chicken coop in Alger, Washington. It was about halfway between where everyone lived. They were able to practice for free during the week. The only requirement of the hall was that they had to play on Saturday night for free for the local kids. These weekly dances gave them experience and the local Alger kids something to do. The snare drummer bought an old beat-up drum set, and the bass player bought a Fender bass guitar on time. Luckily, they all could tune a guitar and play in tune as well. Playing with "out of tune" musicians was one of the things John hated throughout his playing career.

Unfortunately, John was the only one of the four players who could sing and play at the same time. Learning songs and the lyrics was time-consuming, to say the least. Memorizing the lyrics wasn't as bad as writing them down on paper off a purchased record. Once they had about 30 tunes down, John said he would go to the Viking Hall in Silvana and see if they could get a "paying job." John knew they were awful, but … money is money.

Unfortunately, the group didn't have a piano player or a sax player. Normally, every group had that combination of players. Every group Except Johns! John hoped that the Silvana dancers wouldn't notice and would accept his rock'em sock'em singing style. Luckily, the Silvana Viking Hall knew the 16-year-old drummer's family (Scandinavian) and said, "Ya, sure … you're hired," without an audition. John warned the players about the "rough-and-tumble" nature of the hall, and they were able to practice about ten more times before they were scheduled to play Silvana.

When the group arrived at Silvana and set up their equipment (three amplifiers), John was horrified at the band's low volume. He figured the people dancing in the back wouldn't even be able to hear them. John asked the manager of Viking Hall if they had a P.A. (personal address system) that they could use, and he said, "Vats Dat?" So … John put his three-inch speaker amp on the front of the stage with a microphone that could pick up his playing. The microphone was then plugged into one of the other bigger amps (amplifier). John's singing microphone went to the other bigger amp. It was the best that they could do.

The Group was supposed to start playing at nine o'clock, but no one had arrived yet. So … they didn't start playing until people started trickling into the hall. As they played, the dancers just stood around, and some of them shook their heads. This was not a good sign for the evening. As the group played through their 30 songs several times, the crowd started warming up to John's "rock'em sock'em" style. However … the people in the back of the hall didn't dance too much. There was no sound in the back. No loud music. So, the next week, the group had to go out and buy some better equipment … on time.

Little did they know that this was the start of a 3-year career that allowed all the members of the group a fair amount of

"Jack" (money) each month. Later, the group added a trained classic piano player and trained him to play rock. They also acquired a sax player who walked right in and took his place. John was still the only singer, and he had to learn all the songs. Plus, John then had to teach each player how to play their part.

After three years, and 1964, John heard some crazy group out of England called the Beatles. They sang great harmony like the Everly Brothers, and they played by using simple folk music chords. John could tell that they were the wave of the future and suggested the group should change its direction from rock'em sock'em to a harmony singing group. This was not well received by the guys. They were comfortable with what they knew and the gigs that they played on a regular basis. So, John picked a couple of Beatles and Rolling Stones tunes that were kind of the band's current style. John was hoping to make a gradual change for the group, but … they resisted any change. John started getting mad, and before you knew it … they replaced John with another singer and a better guitar player. This was a big shock because John did everything and used his meager band pay for his college food!!!

At this time, John's life consisted of living in a $30-a-month room and barely getting by. All the other players in the group lived at home with heat and "home-cooked" meals (mommy). After John was fired, he had to exist on two hotdog wieners and a can of 10-cent spinach per day: OUCH. He had to shower in the men's gym at school and wash his hair with Ivory Soap. Somehow, he made it through his Junior year at Western and went home for the summer (mommy).

In the early summer, John got a call (two long and three short rings) from a country western singer who needed a guitar player. His group was replacing a former act that left town to promote their record. The singer who left town was named Loretta Lynn.

There were a bunch of taverns on the Canadian border where Canadians could come across the border and "drink and dance." At that time, it was illegal in British Columbia for a business to offer "booze" and dancing in the same establishment. Canucks would have to drink in one place and cross the street to dance at another place. These business regulations controlling the use of alcohol were commonly known as "blue laws." Blue laws are laws designed to enforce religious standards. The word blue was used in the 17th century as a disparaging reference to rigid moral codes and those who observed them. These political individuals were called the "blue-stocking," a reference to Oliver Cromwell's supporters in the English parliament of 1653. Clear up to 1965 many American states prohibit selling alcoholic beverages for on-and-off-premises sales in one form or another, especially on

Sundays. Blue laws allowed forms of retail liquor activity on days other than Sunday. Washington State prohibited the sale of "hard liquor" in grocery stores up until 2014. Even today, a Washington restaurant cannot serve beer if there are "so many" feet next to a public school.

So, the Canadian blue laws of no "drinking and dancing" in the early 1960s was a "boom" for American taverns and bars just across the U.S.-Canadian border in little towns such as Blaine, Washington. Loretta Lynn got her start in one called Bill's Tavern. When she and her husband left for Nashville to promote her records, the act that was hired to replace her hired John to play guitar. He didn't know "country western" music but was able to pick it up in a couple of weeks off of records. John now had the opportunity to "eat" during his Senior year at Western Washington State College.

The first country song he learned was "Hello Walls." John didn't know that Willie Nelson had written it. He only knew the singer on the record was Faron Young. The Canadians, Canucks, could not get enough of American country western songs, and so Bill's Tavern was filled every night that he played. The pay was Okay, but Bill's Tavern had a "fringe benefit" of allowing the band to drink all the beer they wanted for free. John certainly got his fill of beer at age 20, even though he was underage. John learned lead guitar work for about 50 country tunes and got to play guitar solo work for such songs as Lonnie Mack's recording of Memphis. He also discovered that Canadian ladies like the musicians that are up there on stage and wanted "to meet them" in the parking lot. It was a crazy Senior year, BUT somehow, some way, John was able to graduate in June of 1966.

For graduation, John picked up his "cap and gown" from a college store and then went home to get his parents for the graduation ceremonies the next day. When John arrived, the house was surrounded by cars owned by various relatives. WOW, he thought, a graduation PARTY for me! When John got out of the car, his dad came out with a stern look on his face and said, "Cora has died", and walked back into the house. John's beloved mother, Cora, was dead. He just stood there and started to cry. He went out to the edge of the bluff and cried for a long time. Going from a real high (graduation PARTY) to a real low (Mom's death) had a severe effect on him for the next month. John was able to play at Bill's Tavern, but he didn't go out to the parking lot. The free beer FLOWED.

Later, John got his college graduation certificate in the mail one day and his 1-A draft classification from the draft board the next day. The Vietnam War was going strong. The rich kids were able to finagle getting out of the draft, but John was not rich; he was "toast." John decided to work weekdays at the frozen food factory and Bill's at night until he was drafted. It was only two months later that he got his "GREETINGS" notice from the draft board. John was ordered to report for induction into the Army at Mt. Vernon, Washington.

Chapter 7 – Raise Your Right Hand

As John's dad drove him to the draft board for induction into the Army, John's thoughts were going a mile a minute. Two years of his life in the Army! What was going to happen? Was he going to Vietnam? Would he still be alive after two years? John's father, Noel, could see it was time for some Fatherly advice.

"You know, John, you will be okay." John had heard that phrase ever since he could remember; "John will be okay!" Dad continued. "With your college degree, you will probably be taken out of the infantry." Yeah, but what will I end up doing?" John grumbled. His dad continued, "Don't ever volunteer regardless of what you are told. Volunteering will get you doing extra work, extra duty."

The drive to the Board seemed like an eternity. They pulled up in front of the draft board office and got out of the car. John grabbed his suitcase, and one of the draft board "volunteers" said, "You won't need that. You only need the clothes that you are wearing."

"Not even underwear?" John replied.

"That's right. The Army will supply everything. All your clothes will be "General Issue." That is why you will be known as a 'G.I.' while serving your country."

So, now, I am a G.I: General Issue? thought John!

There were 30 guys (G.I.s) standing around, and they were herded like cattle into a small room. The Draft Board employees gave them an endless amount of paperwork to fill out. John didn't know it, but paperwork would become his saving grace for the next two years. Some of the guys couldn't read well. So, a few of the G.I.s helped them fill everything out. When they were finished, the Board employees herded them outside to wait for the Army bus.

After two hours of standing around (Hurry Up and Wait), an old ugly green school bus showed up, and they all went on board. A sergeant sat in the front seat, and he said nothing as the recruits took their seats. Once the bus started moving with everyone aboard, the sergeant stood up and began to explain, in a calm voice, what was going to happen.

"Gentlemen, you are going to be processed into the Army at Fort Lewis." Fort Lewis was ten miles south in Tacoma, Washington. "You will be given your general issue of clothes and have temporary living quarters as you are processed. Your basic training location will be assigned, and you will ship out sometime next week. Any questions?" No one said a word. UGH!

When they arrived at Fort Lewis, the sergeants ushered them off the bus to a mess hall (cafeteria?) so the guys could have dinner. The word "mess" came from the Old French word "Mes", which means portions of food. The mess hall was serving Mac and Cheese that, in reality, tasted like plain pasta. This introduced John to the non-tasting food that he would eat for the next two years. As the new recruits walked through the food line, a guy in front of John grabbed a small salad, and a cockroach jumped off it. He yelled at the cook standing behind the food station, "Hey, there was a cockroach on my salad." The cook just looked at him and said, "Don't worry. He doesn't eat much."

After breakfast the next morning, it was time to get their "general issue" of clothes. The first thing they gave was a large duffle bag. The recruits were informed that this duffel bag was now their closet, and it would hold their G.I. clothes. As the guys changed into their Army clothes, the sergeants seized their "civies," their normal civilian clothes. The sergeants calmly wrapped their civies up in brown paper and had them sent back to each recruit's home address. Then they took the guys to the post barber and completely cut off John's "Beatle haircut." John was now truly "General Issue," a skinhead. Now all he possessed was Army green everything! This included his boxer shorts, the dress jacket, and the cap that was issued to John. *Lovely.*

They then moved them to their temporary barracks. After assigning all the recruits to an alphabetical bunk bed, the sergeants had everyone leave everything in the barracks, and they herded them onto another building.

"Gentlemen, take off your clothes and get into your skivvies!"

"What is a skivvy, sergeant?" asked one of the guys.

"Your underwear!"

It turns out that they were going to examine each one of them with a quick medical exam. The sergeants told everyone to get in a line and follow instructions.

When it was John's turn in line, they shoved a stick down his throat and barked at him to say, "Ahh." The next examiner he came to grabbed him by the balls and said, "Cough." John thought, "This is crazy". They checked his heart and lungs with a stethoscope and said to get in the "line over there." Now what?

As the second line moved forward, one of the guys three people up in front of John, "fainted" on the floor. They picked him up and placed him on a folding chair. John couldn't imagine what was next for him. As he got closer to the action, John could see they were giving medical shots to each person without a warning in advance. The guy who fainted had suddenly seen the needles sticking in his arm and fainted. John walked forward, got jabbed, and it was over. "Wow, this was Army life?"

When the recruits got back to their bunks, John laid down to take a nap. He was always able to nap anytime, anywhere. This was especially true in college when he worked nights and took an 8 AM class required for graduation. He had often taken a nap at the Western Library, laying his head on a desk. As John lay on the bunk, he thought it felt pretty comfortable compared to his old WW II Navy bunk back at the cabin on the island. He fell asleep until a sergeant came in and started yelling that they all had one final requirement for the day. He said the guys had to take a series of small tests. The sergeant said the tests would show what areas of skill each recruit had that the Army could use. The tests were on subjects John had absolutely no experience in. This included auto mechanics, electronics, repair work, assembly procedures, etc. However … John did the best he could on all these tests because he didn't want to go into the infantry.

After this day of becoming General Issue, the recruits now had to kill time until their basic training assignment was given and then "shipped out." They lay around the barracks and had nothing to do for days. Unfortunately, the Army took all their personal belongings, such as books and "civies." After about three days, the sergeants woke them up early and told them that we were "shipping out" for basic training at 0900 hours. One guy asked where they were going, and the sergeant said, "I have no idea, but it will not be here at Fort Lewis." Fort Lewis was a huge basic training facility, but the Army wanted new recruits to leave their normal surroundings for basic training.

Everyone got on a bus at 0900, and they were driven to McCord Air Force base next to Fort Lewis and they boarded a jet airliner. John had never flown before, so he was excited. The sergeants organized them throughout the plane until it was completely full of G.I.s. There were three cute stewardesses who stood and watched. After the guys were seated, one of the stewardesses announced, "Welcome aboard. We will be flying to Fort Hood, Texas and landing at Gray's field next to the base. The flight should be less than three hours." The stewardesses obviously had done this before and knew the procedure. John noticed that these flight attendants looked at them with kind of sad eyes. They knew what some of them were in for. Some hard times in Vietnam. It was apropos that Fort Hood was next to a town named Killeen.

The recruits proceeded into Basic Training in October, which would allow them a two-week break in the middle of training for Christmas and New Year's. When the time arrived, getting home would really be a problem monetarily! However, one of the guys from Colville, Washington, had a good idea. He got seven of the guys from Washington State, including John and rented a nine-seat station wagon.

The idea was to use the rented station wagon and drive non-stop to Washington State. Then they would drop each guy at their hometown?"

The seven recruits checked into the estimated rental cost and discovered that it would be $22 a piece plus gas at 25 cents a gallon. Why Not?! So, they rented the 9-seat station wagon, bought $10 of auto insurance $50 of beer, and took off! Each of them would take a two-hour driving stretch, no matter their "condition." They didn't even stop to pee. They just urinated out the back car window so that they could crank down while moving.

When they got to Colorado, one of the guys said, "Hey … this is Colorado. They make a beer here that I hear is pretty good. It's called Moors or Toors … or something like that."

So, they stopped at a liquor store, and one of the sober guys went in and asked for Toors beer. When he came out, he had a case of something called Coors Beer. "Wow … it was pretty good. It was certainly better than the military non-label beer that they had been drinking."

Once in Washington State, they started dropping the different guys off one by one at their home destination until

John was the only one left in the car. This was great because he got to take the station wagon home and use it over the holidays. John went up to Bill's Tavern and looked up a couple of the girls. It was a great holiday, but before he knew it, he had to start driving back and picking up the guys in their hometowns. Little did John know that the estimated rental fee for the seven of them was based on a mileage estimate by the rental car company. John went 500 miles over the total estimate with all his personal driving. When they all got back to Killeen, Texas, with the car, the mileage overage required another $50. John didn't have any money due to the fun over the holidays. So, all the guys "chipped in." John now owed money to the six guys! His pay was $72 a month, but he was able to pay them off one at a time over the next three months.

All the recruits finished basic training in late February and graduated. The next morning at rollcall, the sergeants started "yelling at them." The sergeants were to tell them where they were headed too next for their unit assignment.

"The following will report to the 2nd of the 41st Armor Unit, 2nd Division, Fort Hood, Texas. Acronson, Jamison, and Kennrick." And then it came, "Wagner."

WOW, John was out of the infantry. He received orders to report to an Armor (Tank) Unit there at Fort Hood. His orders said that his "military occupational specialty" (MOS) number was "63-B-30. "What the heck was that?"

It turned out that every G.I. is assigned a "military occupation code", and John was 63-B-30. He asked one of the basic training instructors what that was, and the instructor said, "I don't know. I'm a 64-A-4 myself."

So, John walked to the Armor unit with his closet (duffle bag) and reported for duty in the "orderly room." This is where each unit does its administrative work and keeps its unit records. The clerk asked for John's orders, and the clerk took down the information that he needed to assign John to the unit. John again asked what job he would be doing as a 63-B-30, and the clerk looked puzzled.

"I think you're a cook? Maybe in supply? I don't know your MOS number."

So, John went to his assigned barracks, selected an empty bunk, and wondered what the heck he was going to be doing. Then, a guy came into the barracks with dirty fatigues (work clothes) and stinking of diesel oil. John asked if he knew what MOS # 63-B-30 was, and he said, "That's what I am!"

"Oh no! What occupation are you?"

"A diesel engine track (tank) mechanic!"

John immediately began to panic. He didn't know anything about auto mechanics, let alone tank mechanics! John thought,

"This unit is going to find out! They're going to reject me! They're going to send me back to the infantry! I'm going to Vietnam!"

When the unit mechanics started coming into the barracks after work, John discovered they were from all over the country. Ratski from New Jersey. Dennis from Kansas. Carson from L.A. Cuomo from New York State. However, they had one thing in common. They knew auto and truck mechanics AND Now Tank Mechanics. John knew NOTHING!

They took him to the unit's Mess Hall, and they got their food. As they sat down to eat, Ratski, who was the most outgoing, asked John.

"Where ya from?"

"An island in Puget Sound, Washington."

"Aah."

They all ate a little bit, and then Ratski spoke again.

"Hey … how ol was you when you stole your first car?"

John immediately got uncomfortable, "I never stole a car!"

"What …? Ya never stole a car?!"

"No!"

Ratski stood up in the Mess Hall and started yelling.

"Hey … Hey … This guy here! He NEVER STOLE A CAR!"

John wanted to crawl under the table, but the other guys joined the conversation.

"Ratski! Knock it off. He's not from New Jersey. He might have stole a boat off his island, but not a car."

The next day, after breakfast and straightening their barracks, the mechanics walked to the motor pool where the jeeps, trucks and … TANKS were parked. Boy, John was nervous. When would they find out he didn't know anything? The first day was just introductions and being asked a few questions that he answered as best as he could. John met the motor pool sergeant, Sergeant Sanders. The second day was different. As John walked into the motor pool office, Sergeant Sanders grabbed him by the arm.

"Let's see what kind of work you can do, Private Wagner!"

He took John to a Jeep trailer and said, "I want you to pack the wheel bearings on this trailer."

John started walking slowly around the trailer a couple of times, hoping Sergeant Sanders would leave. He wanted to ask for help from one of the mechanics working nearby. But … Sanders just stood there and got a little impatient.

"Well, get to work!"

As John walked around the trailer, he was thinking, "Wheel bearing, wheel bearing." Finally, John went to basic physics and realized that the "wheels" got their "bearing" from the

trailer hitch. Wherever the hitch went, the wheels went. So …
he started disassembling the trailer hitch.

"What the hell are you doing!?"

"Ahh … I'm disassembling the bearing for the wheels (the
trailer hitch), and I'm … going to go pack it for shipping?"

"You DON'T KNOW ANYTHING … do you?

"Ahh … no."

"Those *)&*^&%* ! They did it to me again! Your day is
through, TROOP. Go back to the barracks while I figure out
what to do with you!"

John thought he was heading to the infantry. He was a little
frantic, wondering what was going to happen. Unbeknownst
to him, when a "G.I." is assigned an MOS number, he is stuck
with it. So, John was a 63-B-30 Track Mechanic no matter what
work he did. This is why Sergeant Sanders said he had to figure
out what to do with him.

The next morning, John walked to the motor pool with the
guys, and Sergeant Sanders asked if John knew how to type.
John told him, "Yes," and Sanderson sat John down at a desk.
Sanderson said to type up a mechanic's handwritten reports on
each vehicle's logbook. Each vehicle had its own logbook
regarding that vehicle's use and repair. This would include each
tank and each jeep. Basically, the vehicle's complete repair
history. Once typing up the status of each vehicle's

information, each vehicle record was then filled out on the 2nd Armor Division "readiness" report. This division report showed all the vehicles of each unit that were ready for combat at a moment's notice. The readiness report was then sent to the Support Command for the 2nd Armor Division. John was now a "track mechanic" who did typing! John's dad had the same problem when he was in the Army. He had the MOS number for a "mule groomer" taking care of mules even though he ran an Armed Forces Radio station in Southern China.

After typing and compiling the unit's "readiness reports" for a number of months to Support Command, John's unit had a surprise inspection from Support Command. John noticed that the inspectors zeroed in on his reports and the "typed logbooks" for each vehicle. Most units only had handwritten vehicle logbooks. Before he knew it, John had orders to report to Headquarters and Band, Support Command, 2nd Armor Division, Fort Hood, Texas. He was being moved out of the Tank unit to a headquarters unit as a clerk typist. Sergeant Sanders was upset again.

"Those)(*%&%(&^ did it to me again!"

John was now an official typist for Support Command, Headquarters and Band. He ended up staying there for the duration of his two years in the Army as a draftee. It was a good duty, and John was fortunate in that he did not have to travel around the country or go to Vietnam. John just "did his time" requirement as a young man required by his draft board and the Army.

John's new unit, Headquarters and Band, had the 2nd Armor Band in it. The band members performed at ceremonies around the fort. They would perform at least three times a week and sometimes eight or more. The players in the band were highly professional musicians who had volunteered (enlisted) to join the Army as musicians. Naturally, John got to meet them as individuals in the barracks and talk about their music careers in their hometown. This varied from New York City to Mizpah, Minnesota. Some were gifted jazz musicians. Some had just played their instrument in a high school band.

Later, going on leave, John was able to fly home on military flights on a stand-by basis for free at a nearby Air Force base. While on leave, John bought a two-door 51 Pontiac Chieftain for $300. Then he drove it back to Fort Hood. One of the guys in his unit named it the "Phantom Rat Barge." A huge car. John also brought back his guitar and one of his big amplifiers with him. The Super 8 was just sitting at home and melting. John knew it couldn't make the 1,000 miles to Fort Hood.

There was nothing to do in the middle of Texas, so John took to his Fender guitar and started teaching himself several different guitar styles that he had heard in Texas. Especially the sounds that he heard in Austin, Texas, on the weekends. Austin was the home of Willie Nelson, as well as some of the rock bands coming into creation during the late '60s. After about six months, a strange thing happened.

"You wouldn't want to play guitar with a Black Group … would you?" One of the 2nd Armor band members was trying to gain John's attention. John wasn't sure what he had just heard!

"What did you say?"

"You wouldn't want to play guitar with a black group … would you?"

John didn't know what to think, "What do you mean?"

"You wouldn't want to play with a black group … would you?"

"Well … I guess I would, but I don't know much about Soul Music?"

The black musician told John, "There's a group in town that needs a guitar player. Their … guitar player just up and quit. "

Do you know any Soul tunes like Marvin Gaye, James Brown, Smokey Robinson …?"

"Ah … no … but I am sure I could learn. Can you get me some records to learn by?" John's old standby of learning songs off of records was going to be tested once again.

It turned out this group was called the Regents, and they were stuck in the middle of Texas with a quitting guitar player. Their player had quit and was going home. Luckily, they had a singer, so John only had to learn the guitar parts, NO Lyrics. So … off the records that they gave him, he learned to play songs like The Horse, Grass'n in the Grass, Watermelon Man, The Tighten Up, and a bunch of soul songs that were mainly chords. This was a trial by fire. John had to put everything together in a week because the quitting guitar player only gave the group a week's notice. In addition, he was not willing to teach John any of the songs. John thought there must have been some "bad blood" or ill feelings within the group. The black guitar musician also asked John if he wanted to buy his big box Gibson L-5 guitar for $500. It was beautiful and sounded wonderful. So, John borrowed some funds from "guys" in the unit with the understanding of paying them back over the next couple of months.

The name of the club where the Regents were booked was called The Scene. The next week, John pulled up to the club early to practice and ready to play. Some of the band members met him at the door and helped John enter carrying his big

amplifier. As John walked to the stage, he stopped and …
looked around. Except for the bartender, John was the only
white guy in the place. The group immediately gave him the
nickname of Que Ball.

John noticed that all the people in the club were staring at
him … he wondered why. The players were very friendly and
helpful AND tried to get him to relax with the surroundings.
They immediately put him to work, going over some of the
material and making suggestions. It did calm John down. He
could tell the audience was skeptical about this "white guy"
playing THEIR music, and … so was John!

The group had a horn section made up of a trumpet, two
saxes, and a trombone. The rhythm was provided by the
standard bass guitar and drums. No keyboard. John was going
to be the only person playing chords for the group. By the time
they were done practicing, the place was packed. Luckily, the
group leader wanted to start up with a song called "The
Tighten Up." John had a featured guitar part, and … away he
went. The players in the group started looking at each other
and smiling. They thought it sounded just like the record. They
didn't know that that was John's strength. Song after song
sounded "just like the record." The crowd hit the dance floor,
and everyone was happy with John's playing.

When they finished, at 2 AM in the morning, all the players started thanking John for playing with them. Great, but John had to ask, "What is the pay?" The leader came over and said, "$10 a night to start." He could tell John wasn't happy, so he said, "Well … maybe $15 a night to start with raises coming in a couple of weeks? It depends on how many new songs you learn and play well."

The next morning when his Army unit's Reveille bugle sounded for Army Roll Call at 5 AM, John could tell he didn't get much sleep. John had a hard time just putting on his pants and coat to go outside and salute the flag as it was raised. When Reveille was over, John crawled back into bed with instructions for his bunk neighbors to wake him before they went to work. John must have drunk a pot of coffee at headquarters that morning to get moving. Somehow, in some way, he made it through the day and in time to play at the scene that night. Some of the players and the singer gave him some more songs to learn off of "their records" that they had found. Ouch!

After a couple of weeks with the Regents, John settled into a groove with the group. John had to admit it was one of the most "fun gigs" that he ever played. The music was fairly simple, and he was appreciated by all the involved people because John played songs "just like the record." However, there was one exception for the records they gave him: James

Brown. His guitar player and the rhythms James Brown came up with were so unique John could never grasp the exact sound of a record. He could certainly play some of the chords and the beats. He came up with a sound that was similar. Luckily, John's "version" of James Brown allowed the singer to sing and the dancers to dance to James Brown's songs there at the Scene.

After three months at the club, the group had saved enough money to get out of Texas and head home to Atlanta. They thanked John for his "help." They had been stranded without a guitar player. After they left, John never saw them again. However, John will never forget "2 Shoes" Johnson, "Doc" Watson, Harvey, and the other players. John made sure that "Que Ball" told them how he appreciated the time playing with them.

Two weeks after the Regents left, a weird-looking guy came into John's living quarters "looking for the guitar player." This guy looked weird! He wore the craziest-looking red-tinted glasses and civilian clothes that made him look like a "hippie." He said he only had four months left in the service and wanted "to stay sharp" playing his bass before going back to San Francisco.

"Would you be interested in jamming for a couple of hours a day?'

John told him he wasn't that interested in playing "for free" just so the musician could keep his "Chops (ability) Up." The weird guy wasn't that surprised at John's reaction and said, "If you would learn some San Francisco songs, I will pay you $5 an hour to play with me." John was intrigued.

"You can afford to pay me $5 an hour?"

"Yeah, I have money in the bank. I used to make good 'bread' before I was drafted."

"What do you mean, bread?"

"Money."

Boy, this was going to be interesting. John said he could learn from any records the guy had. He then looked at John with a big question mark written across his forehead.

"You don't know any San Francisco stuff?"

"No … what do you mean San Francisco stuff?

"Music by the Grateful Dead and Janis Joplin or Jefferson Airplane …"

"No, who are they?"

"Great … what do you know?"

"Top 40 music and the English groups"

"Do you know The Who, Jimi Hendrix, Cream, etc.?"

"Yeah, I've heard of them. I could learn those ... I guess. Hendrix is kind of crazy, but I could learn his basic songs like Purple Haze and Foxy Lady."

The guy accepted John's counteroffer, and he started paying John in cash each day they played together. The guy also told John where he could hear San Francisco songs on the radio, and away John went. Outside of Hendrix, most of the songs were pretty simple to learn.

The San Francisco musician also asked if John wrote any tunes, and John said he had never tried. John was intrigued by that, and the guy told John to write some unique material. So, John tried to adapt to this new type of material and write songs. He had to admit that when he was playing this kind of music, it was the lead guitar work that was challenging. The music style was certainly different and allowed free free-flowing creation of music. This kept John busy for a couple of months until the guy left the Army. John also began to gain some experience in the area of writing "San Francisco Music." He thought the writing of the music material was fairly easy, and he liked doing it.

This time, pursuing this area of writing music caused John to think of "maybe" going to Hollywood when he got out of the Army. Maybe go there before heading home. *Maybe*, seeing what the songwriting business was all about.

Chapter 8 – Hollyweird

In the latter part of October 1968, John drove through the Fort Hood gate with his "mustering out" papers, severance pay, and a full tank of gas. The Phantom Rat Barge was humming, the sun was shining, and he had decided to go to Hollywood first before heading home to Washington State. John had never been to California. He had never viewed the Pacific Ocean. This was going to be exciting.

After six hours of driving, John had to pee. That's when John discovered he was still in Texas! Texas is a mighty BIG state. John decided to go on to El Paso and spend the night. He drove all day, and now it was nighttime. After he drove in the dark for quite a while, John finally pulled into El Paso. Since the sun was starting to creep up over the horizon, he decided to spend the rest of the "night" sleeping inside the Phantom Rat Barge. Wow, Texas is a big state.

When John woke up in the back seat at around noon, he decided to "splurge" and have a sit-down lunch before hitting the road. He saw this place called Leo's and thought it must be a Chinese restaurant. John went inside and sat down to look at the menu. He didn't see his favorite, Sweet and Sour Pork. So, he ordered something called a Pork Enchilada. When John started eating it … Ohhh it was spicy! It was very good but spicy. He asked the waitress what part of China this food came from, and she laughed!

"This is Mexican food, sir."

Mexican? John thought. *Was he in Texas?* As John finished the meal with his nose and eyes watering, he thought, *Boy, this Mexican food was really good!* John decided to lock this adventure into his memory bank. He would eat "Mexican food" again sometime if he could find it in Hollywood.

John spent the day and night in an El Paso motel and drove out early in the morning. The sun was coming up. He was on Interstate 10, and the map said it went all the way to Hollywood. John was thinking he could drive non-stop. This interstate went a bit into the State of New Mexico, and then he could hit Arizona flying along in the Phantom Rat Barge. It seemed both states were just the same in appearance until he hit the cactus area of Arizona. These were the first cacti that John had ever seen outside of watching Hollywood western movies.

By the time John hit the California border, it was getting dark, and he had to stop to get some food. He also got a "few" cups of coffee in Indio, California. It was 11 PM when John got back on Interstate 10 and noticed the sign he was longing for … 127 miles to Los Angeles! The night sky was clear, with stars everywhere in the open desert. John began to daydream of what to expect when he would get to L.A. He knew it was not going to be the Island or Marian. Los Angeles would have excitement and the chance to see if his guitar playing could "cut it" in Hollywood.

Finally, John started driving (and driving) into the Los Angeles city limits. He started looking for a motel sign next to the freeway; nothing. John saw a road sign that said Harbor Freeway. Oh boy, the ocean! The Harbor Freeway didn't have any motel signs either. Then he saw a sign that said Imperial Highway exit. John figured this highway should be like Highway 99 and have some motels. So, he got off the freeway. As John drove on this Imperial Highway, the buildings looked a little ratty. Then he saw a burned-out building; that's too bad. Then he saw another … and … another … and ANOTHER. Oh my God!! I must be in Watts, where there were recent riots in 1968. John panicked and did a U-Turn in the middle of the road and ran every red light back to the Harbor Freeway, heading back into L.A. Then John saw what he wanted to see … "Hollywood Freeway Exit." John figured there must be a motel in Hollywood, and he was right: one on every street corner. He checked into the first one that he saw and went to bed. In the morning, he was told by the front desk that he slept past "check-out" (whatever that meant), but it didn't matter. John was now in Hollywood.

The sun was shining, it was 80 degrees, and everyone was wearing casual clothing. John didn't see a business suit anywhere. Wow, this is great! His mind started wandering as to what to do as he drove down Sunset Blvd. A couple of miles later, John saw a sign off the road; "Furnished Apartments $250 a month." John immediately turned off Sunset and went to a side street called Lanewood. It was a quiet street with tall pine trees and a full block of apartment buildings. There was a second sign in front of an apartment building with the $250 price quote. So, he parked the Phantom Rat Barge and entered the gate to the apartment complex. The place was clean and had a swimming pool, palm trees, and birds chirping everywhere. It was beyond his imagination as a place to live. John signed a "month to month" lease and brought in his clothes to the "furnished (particle board) furniture apartment."

What to do first in Hollywood? Well, John's first line of income was playing the guitar for someone or someplace. He had obtained some work in Bellingham through the Musicians Union. So, he decided to try the Hollywood Musicians Union and transfer his two-year-old Bellingham suspended (military service) membership. John stopped at a phone booth and looked up the address. It was on Vine Street. So, he headed for this street called Vine. John drove past the union building twice until he noticed it back off of Vine. When John went inside, there was commotion everywhere with the sound of various instruments, trumpets, saxes, strings, etc. Then he saw a sign that said membership and went to that room and paid his $32 dues.

John walked around the building and could see multiple "practice rooms" for musicians. There were a couple of big ones, which he figured were for bands to practice. John noticed another sign that said. "The Jam Room" and went inside. About six musicians were playing some old standards and putting jazz leads in the mix from time to time. They were pretty good. When they stopped, they invited John to play, but he didn't have his Fender or Gibson L-5 jazz guitar with him. John thanked them for the invitation and started to head out of the building. Everyone was looking at him like he was some sort of freak. John figured it must be his military haircut, and he was right. Time to let his hair grow back, finally! John came back to the union a couple of hours later with his "big box" L-5 guitar and went into the jam room. He started to play with the musicians that were there. John showed them what he could do, played a couple of his own songs, and got along with them pretty well. John was hopeful that he could get some work.

One of them asked him for his "card", and John showed them his new union card.

"No, no ... your business card!"

John thought, what the heck was that? He told him no and so the musician gave John his "business card." Wow, that was impressive. The musician said John should get some business cards printed up and hand them out around the hall. Okay… something new … business cards.

When John went home to the "particle board" apartment, he noticed that the apartment building was right next to Hollywood High School. It was also two blocks south of Hollywood Boulevard. The next day, John decided to be a tourist and look around the area. As he walked up to Hollywood Boulevard and started looking at the Stars embedded in the sidewalk and the tall four-story buildings, a well-dressed black dude walked up to him.

"Hey, brother … can you spare five dollars?"

Brother … brother … thought John. *What did he mean … brother?* And then it dawned on John, the BROTHERHOOD OF MUSICIANS? "Oh, yeah, you're in the union, right?"

"Oh … Ahh … Yeah, I'm in the union."

"Well … here's five bucks. I'll see you at the hall."

"Right … see you … ahh…..at the hall," and he briskly walked away.

John never did see him at the … ahhh … Hall.

Luckily, John's first lesson only cost him $5. The very same day (on Hollywood Blvd.), he was approached by all sorts of people in "need." One was a woman who hadn't given her baby milk in two weeks. John quickly realized he was in a minefield and had to be careful with everything he was taking in. John had come to Hollywood with about $800 and had to be careful because it was "shrinking" pretty fast.

John was always good about practicing on his guitar. The saying among musicians was "keeping my chops up." John never played loud in the apartment because of the many neighbors. His big box Gibson L-5 was acoustic with a hollowed-out body, so he didn't have to use his amplifier. Still, people on the apartment landing and his neighbors could hear him play. It kind of got around the Lanewood apartment that John was "pretty good." Just a couple of days into apartment living, John heard a knock at his door. When he opened it, a really good-looking guy was standing there.

"I heard you play guitar pretty well. Are you working now?"

John told him no that he had just arrived and was getting his Hollywood bearings. The guy asked what kind of music he played, and John told him pretty much everything.

"Do you know top 40 tunes? I'm a singer and need a guitar player next week."

Next week, John thought. Wow, that would be difficult to get a club act going in a week! John told him some of the tunes he knew, like "Tighten Up," "Grazing in the Grass," "The Horse," and a bunch of San Francisco stuff.

"Do you know Hendricks?"

John said he knew a couple of his tunes, but what did this guy have in mind?

"Well ... I know "Young Girl", "Hello, I Love You", and some Tom Jones and Engelbert Humperdinck songs. Do you think you could play those?"

John told him that that was pretty simple stuff to learn, but he would need the records to learn off of. The singer immediately left and came back with a stack of records and a list of the songs to learn. Luckily, John still had his $10 portable record player. Wow, this is crazy. I have been here for three days without looking for work, and now I will be working "next week!"

A couple of days later, John practiced with the singer's other musicians a little bit and could tell it would be fine. He just hoped that this act wasn't going to be playing at a "well-known" club in town. John would hate to get a "bad rep" after just three days in town.

When John got to the club, he was relieved! It was a little club on the Sunset Strip with about 50 people drinking around the bar. When they started playing, no one even turned around. John now thinks back to the movie The Blues Brothers with

Murph and The Magictones … that was this job. By the 4th tune, however, some people started looking at the group, and some were even smiling. The singer was really good, and John could tell he was feeling his guitar playing as motivation. When the band finished, the club manager came out with a smile, too. The singer talked to him for a couple of minutes and said, "We got the job."

Oh. No. John realized that this was just a non-paid audition. He got suckered into this! Darn. Just to confirm his suspicion, he asked the singer, "How much do I get paid for this." The singer said it was just an audition, just as John thought! *So, at least he got a paying job now? Right?*

"Well, sort of," he said. "It is $10 a night to start, but we will bring in other club owners to come in and hear us."

"Swell … so this gig will (basically) be an audition stage for better-paying jobs. Right?" The singer looked apologetic at him and said, "Yes."

John could see why the singer needed a guitar player with just a week's notice. This was not good. John had to start looking for work. John posted his availability "at the Hall" and started asking around at various clubs on his off night with "Murph and the Magictones." John knew something would happen, and he was right.

After about two weeks of self-promotion, there was a knock at the door. There stood a beautiful older woman about 30 years old who was dressed in a business suit.

"Hi. My name is Shelia Donavar. I hear you are looking for work. Are you working now?"

This little phrase became John's anthem for work; "Are you working?" People didn't want to hire you if you were not working. Let's see, John thought. "I have to be working to get work. If I am not working, I get no work offers. It always seemed kind of crazy to John, but that's Hollyweird and the (then) club scene.

Shelia asked John a bunch of "professional" questions like, "Can you read music?", "What part of the neck do you play on?" "What kind of strings do you play on?" "What type of amplifiers (plural?) do you use?" And finally, "Are you content to be a sideman?" John could tell that this was going to go somewhere by these questions. Murph and the Magictones © was going to be needing a new guitar player; "next week." John told her where he was working, and she said, "I know the place," with a smile. Just as he thought. John was playing the "Dead End Night Club."

On the weekend, she came to the club to hear John play, and when she walked in, the singer kind of choked. He knew her. On break, he told the band to play really well because a

Music Agent was in the audience. John just smiled. She walked out of the club early that night and nodded at John with a smile. That looked good.

Chapter 9 – Here We Go

John was sleeping when there was a soft knock at his apartment door. He stumbled over the particle board chair in his underwear and grabbed the doorknob. John opened the door and blinked to see a cute woman who appeared scared to death of him. John was a little gruff when he said, "Yes?"

She looked over John from top to bottom in his underwear and finally spoke.

"Hi … I am Cam … and … Shelia sent me."

"Oh … okay. What's going on?" John's Marian small-town manners were showing.

Ah … can I come in?"

"Oh …yeah… . . have a seat" on my particle board chair.

Nooo … I think I will stand … this shouldn't take too long … Shelia needs to get you up to speed … She needs you to have a phone, so we don't have to come here … We will get you a phone and take it out of your first paycheck … is that, okay?"

"Yeah, I guess so."

She paused, and so John asked, "Is that it?"

No… Shelia needs you to get some clothes … I have a list … and I can go with you to pick them out … after you get ready."

"Right now?"

Ahh … I think you should shower first … and comb your hair … and …"

"Alright, give me a couple of minutes."

"Ahh … I will wait … outside … in the pool area, okay?" and she scurried hurriedly out the door.

Oh, brother! Do I look that scary? thought John. He turned on the hot water in the shower because it took several minutes for the hot water to arrive, and he washed up, including his (now) longer hair. When John locked the door and looked for Cam. He found her under one of the palm trees by the pool. She looked a little more secure when John walked out with his wet hair. She stood up and asked.

"Do you want to get some lunch?"

"No, I don't eat when I first get up. Where are we going … to get clothes?"

"Nordstrom"

"The shoe store?"

As a kid with his Mom, Nordstrom was a shoe store in Seattle that they went to.

No … they have clothes to … Ahh … I will drive."

They walked out onto the street, and there was this little sports car with the top down. She unlocked John's car door so he wouldn't climb over the side door. She started driving really slowly out of the Lanewood apartment area. Once they got on Sunset (strip), she headed toward the Hollywood freeway and into the San Fernando Valley. There was Nordstrom attached to what looked like a shopping mall.

Whoa … Nordstrom was no longer just a shoe store. It was huge. As they walked into the Men's section, John could tell the sales staff was looking at him with bated breath. They certainly knew Cam. John looked at a shirt that he liked, and Cam said, "That's not on Shelia's list."

John wondered what was on Shelia's list and asked to look at it. Cam took control, "No, I will pick things out for you as we go." She picked out a shirt, and the price tag said $35 dollars. John got upset, "Cam, it is way too much. That's what I earn in two nights of work!"

Well … you will be earning more income THAN THAT! Besides … this is all going on Shelia's credit card …. anyway. John… you are going to be represented by Shelia, and you have to look the part."

After about ten shirts and five pairs of pants, Cam asked, "Do you have a pair of Beatle boots?"

"No … Army boots."

"How quaint! Now, John … you will need to act with a 'little' more sophistication when you are working for Shelia.

You are going to meet some people that will surprise you and who are very socially minded. I don't know what Shelia is going to do about that, BUT you will have to follow her directions. She wants you to meet her for dinner at her place on Monday … your day off."

So … John kept his mouth shut all the way back to the Lanewood apartment. Cam took charge again, "Here is Shelia's address. She wants you to wear some of your new clothes and arrive at 7 PM sharp."

John thought he said thank you or something like that when she just drove off without looking at him. She didn't even say goodbye. John could tell she thought very little of him. Oh well. Money is money. Shelia is supposed to increase his income. He'll put up with anything to increase his cash flow.

After this encounter with Cam, John played it safe and didn't give "notice of quitting" to the Dead End Club band. He wanted to make sure that this thing with Shelia would work … first. At least he got some good clothes from the shoe store … Nordstrom.

John was off all day on Monday. So, he thought he had better find Shelia's place during the daylight hours since he didn't know the area. John asked around at gas stations and discovered Shelia's address was on top of the Hollywood hills.

He located her home, and it was kind of hidden behind some trees.

After knowing where her house was, John started driving there at 6 PM in his new clothes. John had to admit he was a "little nervous." There was "a lot on the line" regarding possible work in the area. John got to her driveway early and parked on the road until seven and then drove up to her house. John knew the Phantom Rat Barge leaked oil, so he parked away from the front of her house. When John walked up to the house and rang the doorbell, Shelia answered the door … wearing a see-through negligee. John froze at the door … thinking she wasn't ready yet(?) … and she asked him into the house.

"Would you like something to drink?"

"Ahh … maybe a beer?

"I don't have beer in this house, John. Would you like some wine? What do you like?"

"Ahh … Thunderbird?"

"THUNDERBIRD … Oh John, you are new to the area," she chuckled to herself. "I don't have Thunderbird, but I guess I have some sweet whites that you will probably like."

She went into the kitchen and came out with a glass of white wine and handed it to him while she brushed his arm with her breasts. Oh, boy … John had never seen a woman in a negligee "in person." Only in Playboy Magazine. He was starting to get "a little excited" with the situation and quickly sat down on the couch. Sheila noticed and said, "Maybe we should eat dinner first. What do you think?"

"Okay."

She brushed on him on the way to the dining room and physically sat him down on a chair. John scooted quickly under the table. She brought the food to the table, and it looked great.

"I hope you like pasta, John."

"Pasta … what is pasta," John thought… it looked like noodles with some white sauce on it. It kind of looked like Mom's tuna casserole. John figured asking questions about the food would "not be cool", so he pretended like he knew what it was … . pasta. She came over, poured John some more wine and rested her other hand on his shoulder. John's body was getting ready for something, and he didn't think it was dinner. John figured that this whole thing must be some sort of test, and he hid himself under the table as far as he could go. As they ate dinner, John started "cooling down" … finally.

Shelia talked shop about what she does and where John would fit into the picture. She wanted him to work as a "sideman" (the side of the stage) and back up (play for) acts that she worked with. Her clients were the stars, and they would be in front of the audience. She said she would pay John a minimum of $100 per performance, but it did not include practice sessions. Well, at least this was better than $10 a night at the Dead End Club.

After dinner, Shelia picked up both their wine glasses, and they "retired" to the living room. She must have asked John a hundred questions and was fascinated with his log house upbringing. John, when looking back on that time of his life, it allowed him continuous hours to practice and learn songs off the records and the radio. Then Shelia asked about any experience he had with reading music and specifically "charts." John said he had played in some big college bands and read music and charts; she smiled.

"Well, now. I think I have some work for you, but it will always be on short-term notice and late in the morning."

With that comment, she came over to him, stood in front, and dropped her negligee to the floor. She was built, and John's body noticed that immediately. She grabbed John's hand and pulled him up off the couch.

"I want to see what one of my assets looks like," she said with a smile. She came in close and unzipped his pants very slowly. Then she went inside and pulled him out.

"Oh … this is a big boy."

She grabbed a hold and started pulling John down the hallway to her bedroom like a dog on a leash. John didn't fight her. When they got there, she started undressing John slowly.

"Now, John … this is going to be a once-a-month affair. That's all. You will not spend the night. You will go home. I will never book you on the first Monday of the month. That will be my time with you."

John was so "blown away" that he didn't say anything. He just looked around her beautiful bedroom and noticed a few "questionable items" sitting around the room. Finally, he was able to speak.

"What are those ice cubes for next to the bed?"

"You'll see."

Chapter 10 – Working In Hollywood

The phone started ringing when John was asleep. "Ah …
Hellooo?!"

"JOHN … this is Cam! Are you AWAKE?

"Sort of … what do you want?"

"Shelia has a job for you at 11 o'clock. So, you must get up
and get moving. Do you have a pencil and paper?"

John clunked the phone down and got a pencil.

"Okay … what am I to write down?"

"You are going to play for the Merv Griffin Show with
their big band. Joe, their normal guitar player, has a recording
session with a singer. The show address is 744 Vine and Studio
A."

After John wrote down the information, he asked, "What
song am I going to be playing?"

"They have their own material and arrangements. You'll be
reading the sheet music that they will give you. They practice
at eleven and perform at Noon."

By now, John was wide awake. "Can I get there a little early
to look over the music? Who do I ask for?"

"Yeah … you can get in early, but I do not know who to ask for. Just ask around Studio A, where you will perform. Any other questions?" Click!

MAN… thrown into the fire with no known songs. Sheet music … could be anything with notes, chord charts, or a combination of both. John was starting to get nervous. He got dressed (in a "Shelia outfit"), bought a bagel with black coffee, and headed to Vine Street. The building was huge and had no place to park. John drove to a side street and parked the Phantom Rat Barge. John opened the trunk and grabbed his big box L-5 guitar that he used for jazz.

When John walked in, the person at the front desk was expecting him. "Studio A is down the hall and on the right. Ask for Mort, and someone will get him for you."

Mort … okay? When John entered Studio A, all the technicians were putting everything together, and he asked for Mort. "Mort? You want Mort? I don't know if he is even here yet. You won't practice until 11 … Has anyone seen … Oh, MORT! Here is your guitar player for today's show."

John introduced himself and asked if he could see the music. Mort said to follow him to the stage where all the piles of music were. He pulled out three sheets of music and gave it to him. John quickly looked them over and … *Ah, Oh,* thought John. What do some of these "notations" mean in the music?

John immediately started asking Mort questions. "What does the notation AUG and DIM mean?"

Mort was surprised and asked, "You don't know Augmented or Diminished chords?"

"I probably do, but I have never seen it written out. Could we go to a piano for a couple of minutes, and you show me what you want me to play?"

Mort looked a little irritated, but they went to the studio piano, and Mort showed John what he wanted. John knew the chords and showed him what he would play, and Mort said it was okay. He then walked off.

John was able to look over the music before the rest of the musicians started filing in. Most of the music was up-tempo, 120 beats a minute, and with chords all over the place. As John practiced prior to 11, he was able to play what they wanted with not too many mistakes. Mort came in at 11 and started giving instructions to various players. Then he singled out John to the orchestra. "Guys, Joe won't be here today, and so his replacement is Jack Wagner ... (Jack? Oh, well). Jack ... just play the chords on the chart. Do not adlib anything. Just play the rhythm and chords."

A technician came over and plugged a chord into John's big box L-5. The Tech turned up the volume on John's guitar and told him to leave the volume control nob alone, that he would control the guitar volume on the "board." John thought, *The 'board'? What the heck was the 'board'?* Before he could ask, the Tech walked away. The band started practicing, and (Boy) the band was REALLY GOOD. John just played in the background as instructed. At the end of the practice session, Mort left and didn't even look at John. He thought, *I guess … I did okay.* But … just prior to the actual show, Mort came over to talk to John.

"Now … there are certain rules around here that you must abide by. DO NOT try to talk to Merv or any of his guests. Just sit in your chair and do not get up. Go to the bathroom before the show and do not talk to any of the players until after the show, okay?" John nodded "yes" and asked where the bathroom was.

This was going to be short and sweet, and … John wondered what pay he was going to make. But … John didn't ask. He would just rely on Shelia and phone Cam later to find out.

The actual show went well, and John was really impressed with Merv Griffin, a real professional. After the show, a couple of players came over, and they talked about music. It turned out that the guitar player that John played for was Joe Pass, kind of a legend among players in Hollywood. Since everyone was paid the same union scale, Joe would get hired for most of the work in the area because he was the best. Guys like John would get the "crumbs." Still, a union gig paid more than $10 for four hours of playing at the Dead End Club.

When John got home, he called Cam and told her everything went well. He asked how much he would get paid, and she said she didn't know. Shelia would send a check at the end of the month with an itemized list of payments from her various "hires."

John had to admit that working for Shelia was pretty easy. She would book him sporadically each week, and John would have a "ton" of spare time on his hands. He started walking everywhere, but not in Shelia's clothes, though. In walking around, John found a restaurant up in the Hollywood Hills called the Yamashiro. The bar was always empty, and it had a great view of the LA basin. He started taking dates up there "for drinks," and it would impress them. At least something was impressive about him. It certainly wasn't the Phantom Rat Barge or his particle board apartment.

John also loved to drive around on the weekdays with no traffic. He went to the beach and saw the ocean. Wow, that was really something. He was expecting lots of people in swimsuits on the beach, but there was hardly anyone on a weekday. John went to the San Fernando Valley and discovered some Mexican restaurants. He bought a $1 map,

"To the Stars," and found where stars lived. He discovered the movie production complexes and the restaurants that workers ate at. In the space of a couple of months, John knew the LA's Hollywood area pretty well. This exploration came in handy because Shelia was sending him to all sorts of hires around the area. John would play at weddings, Jewish parties for boys becoming men, recording sessions for commercials, nightclub replacements for sick musicians, etc. John usually played guitar, but also played bass guitar or keyboard; "Whatever PAID!"

Chapter 11 – Writing Music

A short time later, Shelia sent John to play at a wedding for someone named Jackie Mills. He figured that was the bride. When John got there (Shelia early), everyone was setting up the chairs, tables, etc., for a small wedding. John asked where the band was going to play, and he set up his equipment. John brought his L-5 big box guitar since it was a wedding.

It turned out that Jackie Mills was a man about 50. Was he marrying someone who looked 25? John later discovered Jackie was a record producer for a number of famous recording artists. The wedding was going to be very casual and relaxed. A "good gig." John played all the number of styles that the group leader wanted him to play. Pretty simple. They played for about an hour, and then they took a break.

Immediately, a woman came over to talk to John. She smelled like an ashtray.

"Hi, I'm Janie … I really like your … playing."

John said, "Thank you… So … are you part of the wedding party?"

"No, I work with Jackie on projects for my employer, Driftwood Music. We are a music publisher and sell our songs to Jackie and others in the recording industry. Do you need a publisher? Do you write music?"

"Well ... yeah ... I have written some songs over the years. I am not exactly sure what you mean by published?"

Wrong words. Wrong answer. Oh no, here we go. She gave John that "gotcha" look and started doing some sort of a sales pitch.

"Well ... we can take your material and sell it around Hollywood to the highest bidder. Then, we pay you a portion of the publishing royalty rights as the composer. If you have a bunch of songs that we publish, you can receive royalties on every record that is sold and a few cents every time your song is played on a radio station. Since there are thousands of radio stations, you could be making as much as $100 a day just from 'radio play.' Naturally, you would need to sign a contract with us. Do you have an agent?"

"Well ... Shelia Donavar books me for gigs such as this wedding."

"SHELIA? You are one of Shelia's BOYS?" she said with a big grin. "Hey, Linda! This is one of Shelia's boys! How long have you been here in Hollywood? Six months?" as she started chuckling to herself.

"Yeah ... I think about eight months. She books me a couple of times a week."

"And ... she takes half your money," Janie said with a laugh.

A bunch of the women started coming over to "take a look at John," and he was beginning to feel uncomfortable. Was he a freak? Was he considered a dork? What was going on?

Janie then started softening up and realized how this was all embarrassing John.

"What is your name?"

"John Wagner."

"Well, John Wagner. Why don't you come over to our office, and we can talk … about a couple of things … regarding your music … and see what we can do for you. Here is my card. Bring your best tune on tape, and we will listen to it. Oh … make sure you come before ten AM. Say around nine next Wednesday?" and she walked off. In fact, everyone walked off, and John was left standing alone.

When he got back to his particle board apartment, he didn't know what to think. *His songs being published? Was this a con job?* John decided to ask around and discovered that Driftwood was a viable company, and none of his musician contacts had heard anything bad. So, John recorded one of his chosen songs on a cheap tape recorder and went to Driftwood at nine AM on Wednesday. There was only one car in the parking lot as he went up to the door. It was locked, and so John knocked on the door. When the door opened, Janie was standing there and smoking what smelled like a Camel (strong) cigarette.

"Come on in, John. We open at ten AM so we can be alone … with your tune … until then."

John had a feeling that there were some alternate motives, but he entered into all the cigarette smoke. The place smelled like the Dead-End night club and there were papers spread all around the office. The place was obviously busy with work to be done. Janie took him to a room in the back of the office and closed the door.

"Now, John … I am willing to see what I can do with your material. It is going to be a lot of work on my part … … I expect to be rewarded for MY efforts. Do you know what I mean?" as she walked up to him.

Man … she smelled like an ashtray. John was wondering what he should do. Then she grabbed the zipper on his pants and pulled it down. John had to admit that this always turned him on, and he let her have an inspection. She jumped up on the counter and told him to start going at her. She started screaming all sorts of cuss words, compliments, feelings, etc. John started worrying that someone would hear and call the police, but that didn't happen. He found it hard to climax with her smelly cigarette clothes on and kept going until she told him to stop.

"Whew … Shelia sure knows how to pick you guys."

After they fully dressed, they went out to the office area. By now, it was ten o'clock, and there was another woman typing away. Jannie smiled and said, "John, you remember Linda at the wedding, right?"

Linda looked up at him with disdain and a short glace. She continued her typing without interruption.

"Now, John … let's listen to this song of yours."

John got out his reel-to-reel tape, and they listened to it twice. Janie seemed to be interested in the material. This was a good sign.

"Yeah … this is pretty good, John. I think … I can sell this. Do you have a bunch of these?"

John said that he did, and she had this surprised look on her face. "Linda … I guess we will have your husband put this down on sheet music. Linda is married with two kids. She and her husband are kind of a team around here."

Janie got on her business look and started telling John what to expect.

"Are you part of ASS-CAP or BMI?"

John told her he had no idea what they were, and she chuckled.

"I suppose not. Well ... I think we will set you up with ASCAP. That stands for American Society of Composers, Authors, and Publishers. They will collect royalties for us, and then we will pay you. We will also need you to sign our standard contract. Linda will get you started on your ASCAP application."

Linda tried to smile as she asked John personal questions while filling out the application. Then she "shoved" the standard Driftwood contract that was required of their songwriters, and John looked it over. John had no idea what he was about to sign, but this was an area that simply came out of the blue. John figured he had nothing to lose.

Janie had a rule regarding a songwriter's material. They had to go to the backroom (before 10) for every song that John brought in to be heard and possibly published by Driftwood. Before John knew it, he had ten songs published and being shown around Hollywood by Driftwood Music. Damn ...he hated the smell of Camel cigarettes, but ... what the heck.

Chapter 12 – Hard Rock

The phone rang early one morning when John was asleep.

"Hellooo …"

"John, this is Shelia. I have an interesting situation. You have played rock, right?"

"Ah … yeah"

"Well … I just got a call from the manager for Mega Noise, a local group that has a record out. Their guitar player just quit and walked out prior to a club gig that they will start on Saturday. I know I have you booked for Saturday, BUT I think this might be better for you and for me. It would pay you double your normal pay."

"Do they have sheet music that I can look at?"

Shelia laughed, "No, John, they don't read music. I will have to get you their recordings they have made. You would have to learn off from their record album. You've done that before, right?"

"Yeah, I know the drill."

"This could be a very good-paying job that might last for a couple of months if they can't find a new guitar player right away. The music is pretty stupid, but you won't have to learn any lyrics. You won't have to sing harmony or anything like that. Just play guitar … ah … LOUD! Cam will drop by with their album. See you next … Monday night, John.”

Cam, with her efficiency, showed up an hour later with the group's album. When John listened to it, he could see what Shelia meant. It WAS pretty stupid stuff. They didn't even play in tune on the recording. They must have recorded everything in their garage and sold it to a record label called Dunz Records. John would have to play with feedback from his big box L-5 guitar, like Jimmy Hendricks. When he used his big Gibson L-5, the feedback would be easy to control with its volume control.

Shelia set up a practice, and John was right. It was in a garage with lots of insulation on the walls and ceiling. There were three players: a bass guitar, a drummer, and a keyboard player. When John walked in with clean clothes and a “Shelia haircut,” he could tell these three were going to be a problem to work with. John tried to be civil with general chit-chat as he opened his guitar case. When he pulled out the big box L-5, they laughed and said, “What the hell is that?”

“It's my feedback guitar.”

How did it work? Well, John would hit a note, and the electrified guitar tone would come out of the amplifier. The amplifier tone would be picked up on his guitar pick-ups and go back into the amplifier and back to his guitar, and so on.

This would cause what is called feedback with a "steady guitar tone" out of the amplifier. John would control the distortion with the guitar volume control and his fingers on the neck.

"Well … let's see what you mean!"

The group hooked him up to a huge Marshal Amplifier. John then turned the volume knob on the amp to full volume. They almost talked in unison.

"You'll blow the amp!"

John said, "No," he would control the volume through his guitar and showed them how he did it. They were surprised by the sound that John's L-5 could make. Then, they started playing each song on their album from the first track to the end. By the time they all finished the last song on the album, they could tell that it would work for the club concert. As usual, John was able to play just like their record.

The bass guitar player was still a little obstinate. "I'll bet you think you're better than us, right!"

"No … I'm just here to help you with your club concert on Saturday. That's all."

John could tell they were a little relieved. They were probably worried that John would try to "muscle into the group," but John had no desire to play their music beyond the club concert.

When John got back to his apartment and tried to rest his eardrums, the phone rang again.

"John … this is Cam. I hate asking you, but … … could you play at my church Sunday? Our guitar player had an emergency and went out of town. The service is from 11:00 to 12:30. I know you aren't booked … so …"

"I suppose I could. I haven't played church music in a long time, but it is usually pretty simple. I will just need sheet music, Cam. Just get me the piano music. Can you do that?"

She said yes. So … no Sunday morning "sleeping in." John would play the "concert" Saturday night, then "church" Sunday morning, and go to Shelia's Monday night. Whew.

The church gig was going to be interesting. Cam said it was temporally in an old school gymnasium. Interesting. When Cam hung up, he could tell she was appreciative and even softened a little toward him on the phone.

Saturday evening was on John's "oh no" list. He was not looking forward to playing with those three guys. John was going to ask the bass guitar player if he could "tune" the bass guitar for him. John knew he would have to be very friendly so the bass player wouldn't think John was thinking, "I was better than him."

When John showed up at the Gazzarri's Night Club, there was already a line forming at $10 a ticket?! At least the club had a parking spot for the performers. Parking on the Sunset Strip was not fun. John went inside and said "Hi" to the keyboard player. He totally ignored John. He didn't hear or see John? Oh no. He was loaded up on something. As usual, the bass guitar player just frowned at John. The drummer was building a drum set that was all over the stage. He must have had 20 drums he was assembling. They practiced the first three songs briefly. The keyboard player wouldn't stop playing until the drummer threw a drumstick against his back. John decided to make an executive decision. He started giving orders to the three, and they listened. Even the bass guitar player listened.

When the door to the club opened, a mass of humanity flowed into the place. It began to look like the Silvana Viking dance hall on steroids. John was glad the stage was so high off the floor. No one could sit on the edge. The group's manager showed up and didn't even thank John for "helping out" his band. Real class. The drummer started pounding each of the 20 drums one at a time and tuning them to what? It sounded very unprofessional. When it was time to start, John was the only one on the stage. People in the audience started yelling at him, and he just pretended to work on his equipment.

Finally … ten minutes late … the three came on the stage and got ready to play. Suddenly, the keyboard player started playing the first song, and they had to jump in late. Everything started to sound awful, and so John cranked up his guitar volume and took off. The other three slowly came around, and they started sounding like a $10 ticket group. So … that's what John did for the rest of the first set. He would control and organize the other three a few bars into each song. The crowd was responsive to the high volume and the heavy (20 drum) rhythm.

An hour later, they went on a break in the backroom. Suddenly, someone opened the backroom door and started letting these teenage girls into the room. They looked like they were sixteen and going on twelve. John just wanted to rest, but the other guys started going after them. The bass guitar player pulled one over to the corner of the room and started groping her. The keyboard player invited two to sit on his lap. The drummer kept rubbing up against the rear of any girl that was available. John just stood there and watched. Then, one of the girls came over to him, and John had nowhere to run.

"Hi, my name is Sherry. I really like your "drumming." She thought John was the drummer? She continued, "What is your name?"

Since John was in the phone book as well as the phone company's telephone information service, he told her his name was Jack Wiggins. She then started telling him all about her beauty and her clothes from Beverly Hills. Etc. Luckily, Cam walked into the room, and John saw her as a life-saver.

"Cam, honey, come over here." Cam walked over, and John kept talking. "Cam, this is Sherry. Sherry, this is Cam … my wife."

Cam looked at him, a little shocked, and John rolled his eyes so Cam would play along. She immediately picked up on John's hint.

"Hi, DEAR. You sound really good tonight … So … Sherry … do you always try to pick up on married men?"

Sherry said nothing, backed up, and went to talk to an older man nearby.

"Thanks, Cam. You're a life-saver. I am sure glad to see you." She smiled and handed John a piece of paper.

"Here is the address of our church. The service is in the gymnasium in the back of the Catholic school. The CHURCH music group knows you're coming and wants to practice a little around ten AM."

John was curious, "Is this a Catholic church you belong to?"

"No, we are non-denominational and rent the gym while we get ready to build our cathedral. The church has been saving money for over a year now, and the building committee is starting to look for a location. Pastor Bob is our leader and a wonderful man."

"Okay … are you going to stick around, dear?" John wanted his wife to protect him.

Cam chuckled. "No, dear. I am going home to a glass of wine and then bed."

Chapter 13 - Getting Religion

Somehow, John woke up, took a shower, and was now driving down the strip in the Phantom Rat Barge. He had Cam's sheet of paper with the address of the church location. He knew how to use the LA grid. When John got to the correct numbers for the location, he looked left and could see a school on the next street off of Sunset. John pulled toward the church and looked for the gymnasium. He found a place to park and grabbed his L-5 and smaller amplifier. When John walked in, he could see Cam setting up folding chairs on the gym floor. He walked over to her.

"Hi … where do the instruments set up?"

Oh, hi … thanks John, for coming. I think they set up under that basketball net over there. Are you okay with the lack of sleep?"

"Yeah … it was especially bad last night with the keyboard player so 'loaded up.' Is there a keyboard player with this church group?"

"Oh, YES!! You will like him a lot. I know I do."

John turned and went to the basket area and started looking for an electric wall plug for his amplifier. He couldn't find one. The gym was old. Maybe before electricity? So, John set down his equipment, got a chair, and sat down. As he looked around, he figured the place could hold a couple hundred people with all the bleachers and set up folding chairs.

Finally, a smiley guy walked up with electric extensions and chords and said, "Are you the guitar player … replacing Larry today?"

John said, "I guess so?"

"My name is Vic, and I play the keyboard for the group. Cam said she gave you sheet music, but we are going to do some different hymns today. I will get the music for you. Do you read music?"

John said, "It will be okay. Just get the piano music to me with time to look it over."

Then another guy walked up and with authority. "Hi, I am Pastor Bob, and your name is …"

"John Wagner," and John extended his hand, but the guy backed up …

"Cam said you could play our music." He continued, "Okay … I don't put up with any "shenanigans" during the service and no trips to the bathroom as well."

"Where is the bathroom?" said John.

"It is in the basement. The stairs are over there … Have you ever played church music before? Or have you just played rock and roll?"

John told him that he had attended 5 different denominations and played or sang in choirs since he was 12 and not to worry …

The Pastor continued, "Now … as far as Cam … We really love Cam and want to protect her… Are you two dating, and if so, there can be no affection during the service."

"Anything else … pastor?"

"No," and he walked off.

When the service started, the group began with an up-tempo hymn. Pastor Bob walked up on stage "all smiles" and welcomed all the people. It was impressive with so many attendees. Every chair was taken with people even standing next to the walls. Everything was highly organized, and John could tell Cam "had a hand" in setting up the service and the performance. This was definitely not the Lutheran service John was used to back home.

Pastor Bob was very good. His sermon was about the love of Jesus and the life that a good Christian bestows by helping widows and the poor. He said we would all be rewarded with the presence of God in heaven and his way of life. There was no "Fire and Brimstone." There was no "You're going to Hell" type of stuff that John was used to in attending past denominations.

After the service, Pastor Bob walked over to John, and he was smiling this time. "Thank you, John, for helping us out. I feel much relieved with your professional playing. It sounded very good. Cam was right. You are an excellent guitar player. You can come and be with us at any time. Cam will provide you guidance for any further appearances that you would play for us. Thank you, again!"

Well, that was much better, thought John.

He saw Cam breaking down chairs, so he started helping her. She smiled and said, "Pastor Bob really liked you. I think he wants you to stay. Larry's dad died, so we have no idea when he will be coming back … if at all … Can I take you to lunch? … It's on me."

John felt a little uncomfortable because Cam didn't make much of a salary with Shelia. But he accepted. Lunch was enjoyable. Cam started opening up and telling John about her personal life. She was from Texas, West Texas and came to Hollywood to see another side of life. She did. John explained that it was the same with him growing up on an island and a small town on the mainland. John could tell they were kind of connecting as friends, just friends. This playing and then lunch went on for several months because Larry, their guitar player, didn't come back.

The church and Pastor Bob began to affect John's standard thoughts of religion and the teachings of Christ. He certainly welcomed the preaching of love and help for the downtrodden. "Love thy neighbor as thy self," and "Judge not lest ye be judged." The "sermon on the mount" by Jesus' bestowing "Blessed are they who …" really grabbed John as Pastor Bob explained these spoken words. John became puzzled as to why the five prior denominations he attended just talked about heaven and hell and the actions of sinners. In his small town, the churches didn't talk about the love of Jesus and God, The Father. John guessed that that was why Pastor Bob's church was packed with every service.

Pastor Bob's members were very anxious to have their own cathedral and get out of the gym. The giving was sizable, with all the money and sealed envelopes being put in four FULL laundry baskets each Sunday. Of course, Cam was in charge of the deposits the following Monday. She said the one-million-dollar goal was getting close and would be reached in the next couple of months.

When John would leave church with Cam, they would talk about the loving words of Pastor Bob. Back home, she had attended a Southern Baptist church with her parents and siblings. Her church would talk about the evil of others and sinners that surround us. She found that Pastor Bob's sermons on "loving one another" and "helping others" brought her closer to God. John began to feel comfort and reassurance of living his life through the teaching of Jesus as well.

John was playing with Mega Noise every Saturday night and playing at the church every Sunday morning. When Mega Noise finished for the night, he would sprint out the door to get some sleep. John wasn't into drugs, weed, or groupies. The bass guitar player would give him a dirty look because John thought he was "better than they were," but John just wanted to get some sleep.

During John's time off, he began to write more music for Driftwood Music. He started getting some small royalties, but the royalty amount was steadily growing. John noticed that songs about a person's personal thoughts were paying more royalties than the standard "Bobbie Loves Sally" type of fluff. "Personal thought" songs took more work, but he enjoyed sitting at the Yamashiro bar and writing lyrics on their napkins

Chapter 14 – Cam

The phone rang, and John went over to pick it up.

"John … this is Cam."

"Oh, hi, what are you doing this fine …"

"John," she interrupted. "Pastor Bob is gone … and so is all the money. The police are starting to look for him."

"Oh my"

"Yes, oh my." After a protracted pause, she began to speak. "I have made the decision to go back to West Texas. I need to go home, John."

"Wow, sorry about all this, Cam. I am shocked!"

"Yes, I am shocked too, and I need you to help me … I do not want to go back to Texas as a virgin. I want you to come over tonight … about 7."

"Ahh … this is a little awkward … what did you have in mind?"

"Oh, come on, John. You know what I'm saying. Don't you think I am good enough looking?"

John chuckled. "Cam … you are one of the most beautiful women I have ever known, but this …"

She interrupted. "I see … you want to be honorable … Just forget that aspect. I need you tonight, John."

"Wow … Oooh. 'kay. I will bring over some "takeout?"

"That would be nice … my address is 8787 Shoreham Tower Drive, just off Sunset behind the Gillman Club. See you at seven."

It was already four, and so John had to get moving. He phoned and picked up some "takeout" from the Yamashiro bar and drove down Sunset. As he headed toward the Whiskey-A-Go-Go and the Gillman Club area, John couldn't figure out exactly what was going to happen. Cam didn't like him that much romantically. He found this "Tower" and parked a couple of blocks away. John grabbed the food and then walked into the lobby to find the index for residents.

"Can I help you, sir?" said a man at the front desk.

Ahh … yeah … I am here to see Cam Wiley.

"She's expecting you. Go to that elevator and take it to the tenth floor, unit 1004."

How did Cam afford this place, anyway? John was befuddled as he rode the elevator to the tenth floor. When he got to the 10th floor, her door was already open and there was Cam in a negligee.

"Hi, John. Stan called and said you were on the way up." One look at Cam, and he was on his way up. She grabbed John's arm, pulled him inside and shut the door. She grabbed the sack of food and dropped it on the floor. Cam started trembling and moved into John's body, hyperventilating.

"I want you right here on the floor, John, please," she gasped.

"I have a better idea."

John dropped his pants and then pulled down her panties. By now, she could hardly control herself at all. John moved his hands to her heaving breasts and pushed her gently up against the wall. As he started in, she immediately climaxed, and John had to hold her up. Well, that was quick.

She gained composure, and John tried to talk.

"Do you want to …"

"Shut up, John."

She grabbed his bare butt and pulled him to her body while hyperventilating again. This time, John got inside her and started to move a little when she climaxed again. This happened a third and fourth time. After each time, John would start talking, and she would say, "Shut up, John." He would be able to move a little more inside her with each try until, finally, after about ten minutes, she was exhausted. She slowly pushed John away so she could breathe and gain her composure.

"Let's eat, John."

"Well … you dropped the sack of food on the floor."

She bent down, picked up the sack, and placed it on the dining table.

"John, I'm a Texas girl. Not a valley girl. Let's eat."

She went into the kitchen area and got some plates and forks. The kitchen was about ten times bigger than John's. She didn't say a word and started spooning things out onto the plates. As they sat down, five feet away from each other at a big table, she smiled.

"Was I a disappointment, John?"

"No ... of course not."

She chuckled, "You weren't. I had no idea that it was going to be so great. The closest thing I have experienced is riding my horse at a gallop ... Can I ask you some questions?"

"Sure."

"Does the man climax? I noticed that you didn't."

"Ahh ... yeah. But I figured you weren't on the Pill, and I was not a Boy Scout. I wasn't prepared. I didn't want to get you ..."

"PG?"

"Right."

She looked at John with a vulnerable look on her face, and a couple of tears appeared. "You were looking after me... The next time, I want you to enjoy me, John."

"You mean …"

"Yes."

"Well, I guess I better head to Hortons and get …"

"Some rubbers? Girls have talked about those… Don't you dare go anywhere tonight? You're more fun than roping heifers… Besides, I think I'm safe."

About halfway through the meal, she started eating her food with sexy actions on her noodles and her dumplings. So, John started joining in doing the same. He remembered a scene from the movie Tom Jones where the couple did the same thing. Finally, they both were getting excited with all the dripping food and she stood up suddenly.

"Follow me, big boy." She started walking fast toward what John figured was her bedroom. He was close behind her when she jumped into a bed that was already folded back, and she pulled John on top of her. "John" … was now really excited. He started gently and then slowly picked up speed. As John watched her getting ready to go, he timed it perfectly, and they both went off together. John literally exploded in her with all the foreplay against the wall and the action at the dining room table.

When they completely stopped, John rolled onto his back to catch his breath. Cam got a weird look on her face and sat up.

"Oh… icky … ICKY!

"Sorry about that, but you said …"

"I know. I know … go in the bathroom and grab some towels. The bathroom door is over by the window."

The "window" was floor to ceiling, and John didn't have any clothes on, but … it was at night? He entered the bathroom, which was also floor to ceiling, turned on the light and spotted some towels. John knew that he was "spotlighted" and quickly turned out the light.

They both did the best that they could to clean up the bed, but it was a mess. Cam smiled, grabbed John's hand, and pulled him to the "next bedroom." This went on well into the night, and they finally fell asleep next to each other.

When John awoke the next morning, Cam was out of bed. He could smell food cooking in the kitchen down the hall. When he walked in, she was fully dressed and ready for the day.

"I am making you a frittata."

"A fra what?

"It is called a frittata made with eggs and assorted veggies. You will like it if you like Tex-Mex food."

Tex-Mex food? John didn't say a word about that term. They sat down with the food, and he could tell she was a little ill with ease.

"I'm leaving for home this week …"

John was taken aback, "Even after last night?"

"Especially after last night. I do not want to get involved with … no matter how much I want to … John, I will never forget you. Never. I will be reliving last night many times in the future … I am sure, but I have to go back to the family ranch."

John didn't say anything and just listened.

"I will not be back here. I want you to move into this apartment."

"Cam … I couldn't afford the rent."

"Oh no. There is no rent, John. My daddy's business owns this place and would pay all the expenses. You would only have to take care of the place. Daddy bought this for me because it had a guard … downstairs."

John smiled, "I guess the guard didn't do his job last night, huh?"

Cam laughed a little but quickly gained her business stature.

"This is not something you would have to worry about. I will tell Daddy that I found a caretaker, and he will be glad to accept this arrangement."

"Cam … after last night … are you sure that we can't be an item in this wonderful place?

She laughed a little and said, "If you moved in with me, Daddy would hire a gun … do you know what that means?"

So, they finished breakfast and then sat out on the balcony with coffee. Cam stared out over the Los Angeles basin and wouldn't look at John.

"I do not want to see you ever again. I know that sounds cruel, but I know this is best for me … and for you. You can move in the 1st of next month if you want. Stan, at the desk, will have a key and explicit instructions for the arrangement. Any expenses charged by the Shoreham are to go to Daddy's company."

She got up and grabbed John's hand. She pulled John to the door and wouldn't look at him.

"Thank you … John … now please go."

Now depression set in. John finally met someone he could get involved with, and she was gone. He couldn't believe how wonderful the night had been, and now … nothing. He was going to be Caretaker John.

When he got back to the "particle board" apartment, he sat down with a beer and thought about what had just happened. John was depressed about finding and losing Cam all in one night. Then the phone rang,

"Hello."

"John ... this is Shelia ... I am starting to get a bunch of calls that are disturbing ... who is this, Jack Wiggins?"

Oh, that's the name I give to 'groupies,' so they can't look me up in the phone book and call me. I don't want to get bothered at home."

"Well, PLEASE stop that. I have spent a lot of time building up John Wagner, NOT Jack Wiggins. It will destroy my work for you."

"Ooh, 'kay."

"Now ... with all these calls coming in ... I need you to move in with me. I will protect you from these GROUPIES. I want you to move in this weekend."

"I don't know, Shelia ... I still have three weeks left on my lease here. I am paid until the first."

"WHAT?! Are you kidding?! I want you to move in this weekend, John. You are under contract, and I need to start controlling this mess that you're creating."

"I never signed a contract ..."

"Oh yes, you did! Just a second!"

Shelia clunked down the phone, and John could hear her rummaging through her desk. After about five minutes of searching and cursing in the background, she came back on the line.

"After you move in THIS WEEKEND… we will go to my lawyer and draw up a contract."

"Your lawyer?"

"Yes, my lawyer!"

"Well … I don't know Shelia. You normally take half my money for each gig. When Mega Noise pays you $500 a night, you pay me $200."

"John Wagner! You were NOTHING when I met you. You played at a shit club. You wore shit clothes. You got paid shit. And now, you are saying no to my contract?"

"I just need to think about all this, Shelia."

"Are YOU moving in this weekend or not?"

"Well, not this immediate weekend."

"Okay, okay. We are THROUGH! Just forget about any more work from me. I will replace you with one of the other eight guitar players I have under contract. Don't show up with Mega Noise this weekend … YOU are now REPLACED! I will see that you get no work in Hollywood ever again!" *Click.*

And then depression really started setting in.

John had to go to a place of comfort. He stepped out into a slight rain and locked the apartment door. As he went down the stairs to the Phantom Rat Barge, John bumped into a neighbor.

"Where are you going in this weather, John?

"To the gym."

"Oh, you are going to work out? Is it Gold's Gym or something like that?"

"No … God's gym."

Chapter 15 – Needed Comfort

As John drove through the rain to the Catholic School Gym, John started to whimper with the depression that had come upon him. When he got to the Catholic school, he couldn't find a parking space on the street. So, John pulled into an empty reserved stall in the parking lot.

When he got to the gym, the door was propped open, and John walked inside. As he thought about Shelia, Pastor Bob, and now Cam, John started crying. By the time he got to the middle of the gym, John was sobbing and fell to his knees. John then did something he had never done in his life; he asked someone for help.

"Oh, Lord … I need help … please, help me."

As John stayed on his knees, all the problems that he now faced were flashing before him. His thoughts were going a mile a minute. John slowly began to realize that someone was watching over him … his whole life. John thought it must be God or Jesus. When he was five and lost control of his trike down a hill, something steered him into a small wire fence that stopped him. When he was nine, John flew off a swing and fell into a pile of leaves. When John was 12, he was at the top of a tree chopping branches off for a fort. Then he hacked the branch he was holding onto and fell at least 30 feet through the tree branches to the soft forest floor. There were a number of events like this where he came out of it unscathed.

Doors in John's life would close, but then another door would open. When John left the Tempos to go to college, a door had closed. Then a person recognized John on campus, and he ended up starting his own band. A door opened. When John's band fired him, his food money was gone. A door closed. Then Loretta Lynn quit Bill's Tavern, and John got a job. A door opened. When his Mom died and John was drafted into the Army, a door closed. When John started typing up reports, he got a job as a clerk at Support Command. A door opened. When he left the Army and went to Hollywood, a door had closed. Then Shelia knocked on his door, and a door had opened again. Now, all sorts of Hollywood doors were closing. *What now?*

As John kneeled on the floor of the gym, he heard a voice ring out.

"Are you okay?"

When John opened his eyes, he saw several small children surrounding him. They were staring at him with big eyes.

"Are you okay?" said the voice again.

John stood up and saw it was the teacher for the children that were staring at him. John blinked his eyes a couple of times to face reality.

"I'm sorry. I am fine. I used to attend the church that used this gymnasium. I had to come and pray."

"Oh … yeah … the school heard about what you members all went through."

The kids were still staring at John with big eyes. The teacher continued.

"We are going to have a class now … I am sorry, but you are going to have to leave … If you would like, you can go to the office, and Father Mike would be happy to talk about your situation. He is a good listener and counselor."

"I think I will just go."

"Do you drive an old blue Pontiac? If so, you should move it. A tow truck is on the way."

"Oh … thank you for your understanding." The children still had those big eyes.

As John walked back out into the rain and got into his car, he figured this was not a door opening. The drive back to the apartment was kind of "thought time." Luckily, no one cut John off or gave him a hard time. He probably would have run into them with his inattention.

When John got back into the apartment, it was really now a particle board apartment. It was depressing. He wondered what he should do until the first of next month when Cam …

would be gone. He wanted to contact her, but … John stood by her no-contact request.

As he got more and more depressed, the phone started ringing. John almost didn't answer, but … he got up.

"Hello."

A female voice started in. "Is this Jack Wiggins or … John Wagner?"

Oh, great, thought John, a groupie. "Yeah, this is John Wagner."

"Oh good, my name is Shana, and I work for Mike Stuart."

John wondered who he was.

She continued, "Janie at one of our affiliates, Driftwood Music, told us about you …"

"And …"

"We have been investigating your background through the Musicians Union clear back to Wailin Wagner. Mike heard you with Mega Noise last week, and well … Mike and United Artist would like to meet with you next week."

"Before ten …

"Oh, no … Oh, I see, it's Janie … No … Mike would like to meet with you next Tuesday at two. Can you make it?"

Oh my, John thought. A door was opening.

About the Author

Wil has been involved with writing material as a "ghost" for websites and authors for years. He was able to make a good living. In his early years, he was a musician "scuffling" from job to job and project to project in Hollywood. He decided to write this book about all the people he met there and many stories within the music industry. The book shows The Road from his first guitar to playing for "music stars" as a sideman.